Living the dream...
by Mrs P

To my husband and our three wonderful children... thank you for your daily inspiration!

CONTENTS

ACKNOWLEGEMENTS

Profuse thanks are due, in no particular order to:

My immediate family, especially my husband and our three beautiful, kind and funny boys, who have been a daily source of inspiration for me .   I love you all dearly!

My Mum and Dad for not only raising such a wonderful daughter (Me) but for also being eternally optimistic about everything I do in my life (and occasionally providing us with food from their mini-shop if we run out).

A special thanks goes to my sister Jo, she has read this book more times than I have, offering constructive criticism and support all the way through (even, on occasions at mid night).

My wonderful and *(mostly)* life log friends... I am one lucky lady to have you all in my life!

All of the Mothers and Fathers that are in a similar position to our family, whom I have watched over the years and who have unknowingly provided me with some of the characters and story lines.

And lastly, a special thanks goes to my Grandad... you may be in heaven but I don't know where I would be without the lucky magpies that you send to watch over me every day!

1

There's never a dull moment in our house or a spare one!

I lie in bed with my eyes closed, pretending to be dead for as long as I can get away with, whilst listening to the usual morning scenarios unravelling... initially, it's the sound of the boiling kettle from downstairs that makes me stir. This indicates that Dick has already been awake for a while, as he spends his first half an hour of *every single* morning playing games on his phone, whilst sitting on the toilet. He then showers whilst the kettle boils and brings me up a cup of tea, before tormenting the hell out of the kids in tickling fest, leaving them hyper as he makes a quick decent for work. Mornings are frankly one big rush! John is always the first to be up and about, he dresses and makes his own bed without ever being asked to and can usually be found downstairs, consuming the contents of the fruit bowl before I have even got out of the bath.

Our eldest son Lloyds actions mirror my own, he lies as still as he can for as long as he can, while I draw the curtains and make the bed around him whilst pleading with him to get up, until finally I change my tactics and literally going mad at him instead. He then sits staring at the pile of clothes that I have laid out for him (to save time) for absolutely ages, before attempting to dress himself in slow motion.

While Henry, the youngest, shadows my every move arguing that he's too little to dress himself and that I will have to do it for him. This however is an argument that I usually win, if I threaten to take him to school naked, as I once put him in the car undressed with his pile of clothes next to him, following a particularly bad morning which has now left him mentally scared forever *(but hey ho, whatever helps to get to school on time)!*

We live in a detached house with a driveway to the front and lovely big garden to the rear, on the outskirts of town. Our home was once beautifully decorated but unfortunately having three non-mortgage paying little housemates is now, slowly over time, being wrecked; the walls have grubby little hand prints on them, there are cracks in the floor tiles and nearly all of the door handles have become loose, due to Henry's obsession with continuously opening and closing them.

Our life runs on a series of weekly rituals and as today is Friday, within two minutes of their eyes opening the whole family realises that tonight's is 'Curry Night'. This activity used to be celebrated by just my husband and I, it was our 'little treat' at the end of the week after the boys went to bed. To start our weekend off if you like with an adult meal, before the inevitable party food would take over. Always purchased from the same place, always delivered and always the same order - mine hot and spicy whilst Dick's was rather tame. With mint sauce, chapattis and popodoms as extras.. basically 'The Works'.

Our aptly named cat 'Masala' would occasionally be allowed a small share of the popodoms too, as she would appear as regular as clockwork at the same time as the delivery driver. But unfortunately, as she's got older she tends to throw this type of food up afterwards, usually all over Lloyds deep pile carpet or on someone's bed and so is now permanently banned, much to her disappointment as she hovers around us while we eat, to be rewarded with nothing.

It's embarrassing enough taking her to the vets and listening to her name being called out 'Masala Gooden' without having to explain that she's ill following a curry?!
However with the boys getting older and bedtimes getting later and later, Dick started to look at me each week as though he was seeing which parts of me were the fattest, sizing me up to eat. And so fearing for my life, the kids have been allowed to enter 'the curry circle' too. Dick isn't happy about the increase in expense but is even more concerned that he may have to share his food. So now, whilst I dish up enough food to feed the five thousand, he rushes to pour his sauce *(now very spicy, funnily enough)* all over his rice, so that no-one will want nor can have any of his. My dishes on the other hand are now mild, as I have to share and so curry night isn't what it used to be for me. Subsequently, Friday nights now cost us a small bloody fortune!
I have tried cooking Indian curry's myself a few times but am fixed in my opinion that anything other than a curry from an Indian restaurant is not a 'real curry'! This term 'real curry' always slightly frustrates Dick, as he tries to figure out what goes on in my head. We'll sometimes have a Chinese or tinned curry during the week and on a Friday night I'll justify having our Friday night curry by saying 'Well, Tuesday's curry wasn't a 'real curry' was it'? At which times, I can tell by the look on his face that he's both baffled and annoyed by this statement.
I must confess, we have in the past if the kids were really tired, communicated our curry preferences via text messages and told them the little white lie that we were having a break for a week or so. Then Dick would phone the order through to the restaurant in a hushed tone, whilst I put them all up to bed none the wiser.

This is something I have now vowelled that I will never do again though, as last time I caught John getting the silver trays out of the bin the following morning and licking the leftover contents out of them, he was NOT impressed with us at all and I felt so bad that we ended up having another curry that night and so it ended up being more expensive in the end.

I'm not sure whether I'm proud or embarrassed to also admit what I am about to divulge.. as we are such loyal customers to one specific Indian restaurant, the last time Dick and I went out on a 'date night', we got very drunk. We couldn't get a taxi home for love nor money and so we decided that the restaurant could show us some love back, by delivering us home with our take out curry. God only knows what absolute rubbish we spoke about on that journey? I can't remember, Dick can't remember, and neither of us can remember which driver it was either, meaning that it's now slightly awkward each time that the door bell rings on a Friday night... and so we always send the kids to pay. We justify this in our heads by thinking that this is a great way for them to learn about money / change etc.

Mental note - To remember that what may save you money at the time, could cost you dearly long after the event.

It is a total miracle that Lloyd is part of this feast each week, as he is SUCH a fussy eater, a pot noodle is on the verge of being too spicy for him, half way through one you'll hear him cry out 'Water, water!! Oh my tongue'. Whilst John yells back at him 'Oh my god, you're such a drama queen! You should be more like me, I'm Mummy's 'Healthy Boy', I'm such a good trier' and then an argument inevitably erupts, followed by a physical fight and resulting in both crying.

Saturday's usually entail a kids party. Girls get pyjamas every-time, I'm sure they can never have too many 'Barbie' or 'Hello Kitty' pyjamas. I'm also conscious that, having very few female genes myself and living with four males, anything else I may choose could be too boyish. Boys though are easy to buy for - you can guarantee that they will like either Lego, Minecraft, Starwars, light sabres or Nerf guns and so whenever these are on offer, I bulk buy and put them into our much loved 'Present Bag'.

This bag is much like a lucky dip. The boys riffle through it, finding the most suitable gift for the Birthday child, whilst moaning that 'it's not fair', that they don't have this or that *(those particular items then get moved into the loft and added to their Christmas presents, so that I can blackmail them later on that 'Father Christmas is always watching them')*. I am thinking of changing where I keep this bag though, as recently it was my Birthday and I awoke to find John glaring at me whilst holding a Nurf gun to my head, it was like having a glimpse into the future... which was quite scary! This later turned out to be a present 'for me' *(oh goody)*. From which he had kindly removed all of the packaging, so I couldn't even sneak it back into the present bag but instead had to accept it and it now lives under my pillow.

Mental note - When he forgets that it's mine and stops looking for it each morning, to sneak it into the supplies in their bedroom to get rid of it.

Much like Fridays, we have a ritual on Saturday too... Saturday night is 'Lottery Night'. Each week we pick our numbers on the morning of the draw in an open debate, with each person preparing a case for how they have chosen their numbers and why they should be considered for use. *Sad I know!*

We do two lines, using everyone's input and one 'lucky dip' *(just to cover all bases)* and the transaction is ALWAYS made online, so that we don't mislay the ticket, as we do with a lot of our other 'stuff' on our travels. We have come to the arrangement that all parties should be in absolute agreement with the choices before the ticket is purchased so that we can all bask in self pity when we lose and no individual family member can be held responsible or blamed *(truth be told, I think that maybe I take this more seriously than the others).* When we have won in the past, much to my husband's annoyance, we have all excitedly made predictions on what time the e-mail will come through the following day; our group theory is that the bigger the win, the earlier the e-mail will ping up in my inbox. *Needless to say that there has never been an e-mail waiting for us when we have woken on a Sunday morning.*

This week, I have chosen the numbers: '2' the number of return trips I have had to make to school after dropping the kids off, due to one of them forgetting something *(followed by a lecture about how everyone should be accountable for themselves and their own belongings).* '22' As it has been Lloyds Birthday this week on the 22nd and '45' just because 4 & 5 are my favourite numbers. Quite a boring week for explanations on my part.

Dick has chosen numbers '1' and '59' as these are the lowest and highest numbers. He is obviously tiring of this game now. He didn't even wait around for the final line formations, before disappearing off for one of his half an hour poo's.

After a much longer and quite boring explanation, Lloyd chose: '1' because he came first in a maths quiz at school this week... this will be the ONLY odd number you will EVER encounter from this child, as he has a weird obsession with even numbers. The extremity of this situation was really high-lighted a few days ago, when I caught him counting out sheets of toilet roll, to ensure that he didn't finish on an odd number!?

He then went on to chose '22' for the same reason as me, his Birthday. '26' Something about how he never gets the full half an hour on the laptop when I say he can and '42' because if you add such and such and divide it by such and such then multiply etc. etc.... *yawn!!!*

Henry obviously chooses '7' because he is *(not)* seven. This is his choice every week and as standard, his input sparks the usual amusement from the other two, who begin to ask repeatedly, whilst sniggering "How old are you again Henry?" which after the third or fourth time infuriates him and so a circle of violence occurs.

John chooses: '6' because he is six, followed by '18' the age he wants to be and finally '38' because this is my age and he loves me so much. *Bless him!*

At this point the toilet monsters ears prick up and Dick yells out. "Hey, what about me?" No-one is actually listening to him but he carries on regardless, totally unaware of this fact. "I'm sure I'm invisible to you kids! You only ever want me when you need money or someone to play the Xbox with." Which, I'm not sure is strictly true? He enjoys this activity *far* more than the boys do and so he actually needs them for this, as an excuse for not doing jobs around the house that he should be doing.

I frequently pass Lloyds bedroom door to find that Dick has snuck in there and is playing alone, or on other occasions they are all in there but the boys are just spectators, as Dick he has got so far with the levels without them, they haven't gained the relevant knowledge to join in the game with him. So, with everyone happy and in agreement, this week's lottery numbers are as follows + one lucky dip:

Line One: 1, 3, 18, 22, 42 and 59.
Line Two: 2, 6, 7, 26, 38 and 59.

As usual I get straight online to enter the numbers, so there is no time to get distracted. I am fully aware that I would be in *BIG* trouble if our numbers were drawn and I had forgotten to lodge them.

Next up is the dreaded 'homework time' which, Birthday parties permitting is always completed nice and early on, whilst I still have the whole weekends activities to barter with.   It's endless - there's spellings, maths, reading and at times 'theme' work is added into the mix too.   Or there may be songs to be learnt with no musical direction *(meaning that my renditions are usually boo'ed at, much to my disgust)*.   So, to achieve an 'argument free zone' the work *has* to be carried out separately, meaning that half of the day has gone before we can even think about getting on with anything else. *There's never a dull moment in our house.. or a spare one!!*
The only other homework rule is that Henry *has* to be kept out of the dining room.   This is the point that Dick steps up to the mark, there's nothing he enjoys more than lying on the sofa, playing on his phone for hours on end uninterrupted and not having to entertain any one.   His one and only job is to ensure a permanent streaming of 'Peppa Pig', to keep Henry glued to the spot and he's in for it if Henry is let loose, or if he gets the gist that the other people are receiving slightly more attention than him because at this point, it's game over!   He's up at the table, drawing all over the boys books and artwork leaving them up in arms about how they are going to get told off at school because of him. I say 'drawing', he's actually calling the register in his loudest squeakiest voice, making zigzag markings everywhere.   He's the teacher and we're the pupils and upon request, we are all made to shout out 'here' when our names are called.   Now and again I rebel, by being absent from school and after being called ten times and getting no response, my 'teacher' finally looses the plot and goes off in a strop. *Is that mean or is it character building - I'm not sure which but it is quite funny none-the-less?!*
Being quite a goody two shoes, Lloyd usually jumps straight on to his homework.   If he doesn't though, I just wave the iPad at him and shake my head as though he's going to be banned from playing it and that's all he needs before he's there like a shot.

He's very academic and is naturally good at most subjects but particularly finds Maths a real synch. He whizzes through the pages, rarely asking for help because he's learnt that it's easier not following a recent incident, whereby he couldn't get his head around an equation and so consulted us, his parents, the grown-ups. Unfortunately neither of us could figure out how to work out the problem either but we just *wouldn't* let it go! It eventually resulted in Myself and Dick spending the entire evening trawling the internet, looking for answers and ending up having one almighty row about who was closest to figuring it out and what method we had used. *It is wrong to be secretly chuffed that he has stopped asking us for help with this now though, I always hated Maths at school and I'm obviously still not great at it?*

Up until recently John's homework could absorb the majority of the day and would involve me desperately trying to pacify his 'mood' to avoid a tantrum or a sulk which would prolong the agony even more. I would try to stay as upbeat and positive as I could, smiling until my cheeks actually ached as much as they did when I was posing for my wedding photographs - he just really didn't like anything that related to school or learning. However following the very enjoyable recent summer holidays, where he seemed to do a lot of growing up and a *really* lovely new teacher, this year is panning out very differently *(so far.. PMA... fingers crossed this will continue)*. He now sometimes even beats Lloyd to the table and although everything has to be completed in his order, a small price to pay in my opinion, he causes very little fuss.

Spellings are a nightmare for all and in my opinion a total waste of time! Each week we have to explain half of the words to the boys, or them to us *(I challenge anyone to know off the top of their head what a Groyne is)?!*

I know all about digraphs and trigraphs, which I never knew even existed before having children and now often find myself singing *'two letters but only one sound'* or *'three letters but only one sound'*, whilst swiping that amount of fingers across my eyelids and opening them to find my children glaring at me as if they want to disown me.   We spend time circling the different syllables of the words and try to come up with quirky sayings or songs to help them remember it for their weekly tests.   Ask them a week later if they remember and they don't have a clue. *Nor do they remember any of my songs... it's gutting, my talents are being wasted!*

Today one of my sisters 'Mercy' is coming over for a visit, or 'Aunty M' as she likes to be called.   If one of the kids calls her Mercy, it's usually followed up with her correcting them "Er thank you, it's 'Aunty-M to you!"   We also affectionately refer to her as the 'Kiddie Catcher' too because whenever she's around children her skin becomes alive and her nose itches like crazy *(just weird I know)!*   She doesn't have children of her own but mine adore her and so we try to catch up with her on a weekly basis *(mainly to make her appreciate just how lucky she is to be able to leave whenever she wants).*

She and John are both 'middle children' and as such have quite a bit in common (Mercy doesn't like to refer to it as 'middle child syndrome'.. but it is).   The pair of them have recently set up their own club; once a week I drop him off to her house and they do whatever they do at 'Monday Club', whilst Lloyd attends Cubs and Henry stays at home for some quality time with Dick.

This obviously makes John feel very grown up!   I'm not allowed to escort him to the door, instead I have to wait in the car and watch him go in.   I like it because it allows him to experience something that Lloyd hasn't done before him already, so that he doesn't constantly have to be patronised with 'When I did that, I....' as Lloyd does ALL of the time, for one-up-man-ship.

Aunty-M is during the week an unappreciated work horse for a big company. Her calm, rational personality and good advice naturally makes her everyone's agony aunt too. So she deservedly likes to let her hair down with a few glasses of wine most evenings and much like Dick, she too provides me with quite a lot of entertainment. *Mainly at her expense!* The funniest story and one that still makes me belly laugh now, was from when we were at a 'VE' street party celebration, one bank holiday Sunday. She and I decided to have a race in the kids scooters and having been drinking for quite a few hours, was only really going to go end badly. We heard the countdown... 'Ready, Set, GO!' and we were off! She was quite a way in the lead, her little legs going ten to the dozen, when she glanced back to mock me for being so slow, which was a BIG mistake! Because as she did so, she stumbled, her hands still gripped tightly around the handle bars not letting go and my god, when she managed to stand up, shaking like a leaf and trying not to cry, her face was a complete mess of gravel and blood, the poor thing! But no-one could come to her rescue for laughing, I was bend over in hysterics trying not to wet myself laughing, our other sister and all of our friends were crying with laughter too, while the kids were in a stunned silence, not know how they should react or why we were all being so unkind. Poor Mercy was, understandably, in a state of absolute shock. However rather than taking her to the hospital or anything sensible, as we should have done, we just got her even more drunk, to numb the pain.

It was just as funny, hung-over the next morning too. Every time one of us would look at her, we would literally cry with laughter. So much so, that even she had to laugh, although you could tell that it physically hurt her to do so. But the funniest part of it all was that on the Tuesday morning she had to attend a meeting with all of the big-wigs from work and the council too, and no amount of makeup was going to hide the scabs.

I would have loved to have been a fly on the wall, whilst she lied about how she had got them!

Mental note - To try to act more like a grown up when drunk!

So, the weather today is HOT and the boys have been eagerly awaiting Aunty M's arrival. *(No wonder the flowers are getting confused about when to bloom, the weather lately has been so varied).* I have filled up the paddling pool, they have filled up their water pistols and we all know the plan... which is to call her around to the side gate when she rings the doorbell. Then she's in for it, with a good soaking before she can arm herself.

Henry already has his clothes off and is totally naked *(surprise, surprise).* I watch him as he straddles the paddling pool dipping his tiny toes in to test the water, whilst convincing himself that it's warm, even though it keeps taking his breath away and his little pop belly goes in and out like crazy, as it tries to regulate his body temperature. Within two minutes, he has already pee'd in the water and I've given him 'the look' but can't reprimand him out loud, otherwise Lloyd will hear and go on and on about refilling the entire paddling pool because it has been 'contaminated'. He can no longer share his bath water with anyone, even me, for this reason - even though I have reassured him that, at 38 years of age I can't remember the last time that I pee'd in the bath, but he'll have none of it.

You can see, by the evil glint in the other two's eyes, that the sight of him in the pool is already making them consider diverting from the plan and turning on him instead. So to avert this, I suggest that they hide, to add to the effect, just as the door bell rings.

"Come around, we're in the garden." I shout out innocently.

"Coming." She calls back, unaware of what awaits her.

The boys are sniggering and so I hold my finger over my mouth to hush them. The gate swings open and she breezily strolls through. Looking up and down the garden she is obviously confused, not sure whether she should be pleased or scared that it is so oddly quiet. But within seconds, she realises that she has been lured into a trap, as Henry is pointing to where the other two are hiding, jumping up and down and laughing his little head off. All the while they are glaring back at him, as though they are going to kill him for giving away their location and I know that he's now in for a soaking too, as punishment.

She grins knowingly. "Crickey, it's quiet here, are all of the little people out today? Oh how nice, peace and quiet." And with that, they pounce out from their hiding places and shoot her straight in the face with their pistols and the fun begins! She wrestles the gun off of John. Who, now that an adult has entered the game immediately changes his allegiance and is on 'her team', so that everyone is against Lloyd. In any other situation this would bother Lloyd but in a water fight, he relishes at being the wettest and happily takes them both on. Now and again Henry will get caught up in the cross fire and scream like a banshee, so I pacify him by returning fire on whoever shot him. After about half an hour as the game draws to an end, we finish up with target practice, shooting the tin cans that hang on strings from the cherry tree at the rear of the garden. *These remain, following Johns Birthday party last year , where we recreated paint balling using rubber bullets, boxes and camouflage nets.* Everyone is soaked and shivering, so I hand them out some ice lollies whilst I go and find some towels and dry clothes.

"Can I have two please?" Lloyd asks when I reappear, before finishing the one he's eating and I notice the red dye all around his chattering teeth and lips.

"No greedy!" I tell him, smiling at his cheekiness.

"Please! Just to make it an even amount of evens that I've eaten." He states, as though this should make as much sense to us as it does to him.

"No, weirdo!" I repeat, shaking my head at his odd little character and see that Mercy is doing the same beside me. At this point Dick pops his head out of the back door and realises that he can join us in the garden now without having to get involved - something for which I am grateful, as it always ends up with both the garden and indoors being soaked when he does.   But him and Lloyd are two peas in a pod and have had enough of being outside in the fresh air after about an hour, so give each other the nod and disappear upstairs to play on the XBox.   Within minutes you can hear them both screaming from his bedroom window competitively at each other, to do this or that or they'll get killed.

The other two are the complete opposite, they love being outdoors.   Henry has a little high tech motorised car which he is totally in love with (*and can get quite violent if anyone else wants to play with it*) with the exception of John and both of their little bums fit snugly into the driver's seat together and so this is always the first thing they play with.   Today is no exception, they spend the rest of the afternoon driving around, pretending to be going / returning from work and only occasionally asking us to join in, which allows me and Mercy to relax and catch up on the weeks activities. She stays for a few more hours and when it's time for her to leave she tries to do so on the sly, because she knows the drill as well as me - Henrys car obsession stretches to her car too.   It's a small convertible, not too dissimilar to his own toy car and every time that she leaves, he wants to be leaving with it!   He gets in, plays with the roof, gets his dirty mitts over her well polished dash board and then fastens his seatbelt in protest when she tries to encourage him to get out with false promises of how she's coming back.   All whilst his naked little bum is rubbing all over her lovely clean seats and inevitably resulting in me prizing each little finger off of the door, as she makes a speedy exit to her now very appealing quiet retreat.

After packing away the mess from the garden and having some dinner, at 8.20pm we are as usual all in our positions in front of the television, waiting for the lottery to be drawn. Each of us praying that tonight will be our lucky night, the night that *our* numbers are pulled out as we discuss what we would do with the money if we won just as we do each week. We're all in agreement that we wouldn't want to move home, as we love our house so much *(although I'm not convinced that this would be the case if we had millions of pounds)?* I would make changes to the garden, buy a summer house as well as go on lots of holidays. Dick would like to build an extra floor in the loft space and get a new car. Amongst a hundred other things, Lloyd REALLY wants a hot tub. John wants anything that I choose for him *(arh)* and Henry doesn't want for much at all... just 'hot shaky milk'.

But, after the big build up it's the usual outcome and so the boys go to bed slightly disillusioned, their dreams shattered for another week. At which point I consider, as I do each week, whether we should stop them from watching the programme and whether it's healthy to keep raising their hopes each week. But as usual, by Sunday morning they have totally forgotten their disappointment and are already thinking of numbers / arguments for choosing next week's numbers, whilst tucking into their salmon and scrambled eggs. And so the weekly cycle begins again.

2

If I ever needed a week to win the lottery, this would be it!!

After a lovely weekend, Monday morning has come around *way* too soon for me and judging by the looks on everyone else's faces and their inability to find Dicks tickle fest amusing, we all feel the same way.   Lloyd sits and gazes at his clothes for longer than usual and screams at the other two when they taunt him that they are dressed and he isn't. Breakfast is a sparring session that I try to diffuse by shouting warnings from the bathroom, where I am adjusting my make-up, after jabbing myself in the eye with my mascara brush.   And then comes the argument of who's sitting in the front.   Lloyd opens the discussion, as usual, fully aware of what he is about to start and well in advance of leaving the house.

"It's my turn to sit in the front today Mummy."   He says really fast, so that no-one can interrupt him.

"No, it's my turn to sit in the front *actually* because I sat in the middle last night and you were in the front."   Says John, who has obviously rehearsed this in his head already, knowing that the conversation would inevitably come up.

"No actually.   Daddy was in the front last night, derrrr!" Lloyd snaps back at him confidentially and John undoubtedly already knows that he is going to lose this agreement because thinking back, Lloyd is right.

"I know but I'm telling you, yesterday morning YOU were in the front and so it's my turn!" John argues, using a different, less convincing technique now.

And on and on it continues. The total unimportance of this in my life means, that every day when the row erupts *(and I can be damn sure it will)*, I rack my brains trying desperately to remember who sat in the front last and an incident that occurred en-route, to spark their memories to remember too.

So today I award Lloyd the privilege of sitting in the front, which I think to myself is probably best as he is worst mood and so this will cause me the least amount of grief.

However on hearing this news, John is instantly in floods of tears *(oh my goodness, how wrong could I be)*, he begins screaming at everyone about how unfair his life is. I try to stay calm, counting to ten in my head as I feel the anger at their bickering rising inside of me.

He moves his mood into the bathroom, so that he can physically watch himself crying in the mirror and the moaning gets louder and more dramatic as he plays the scene out to himself. We are now running late and I am on the verge of losing the plot.

I usher everyone to the car but John is still crying at the mirror, so I go back inside and stand in the doorway to the bathroom, watching him whilst trying to portray someone that is very much in control of the situation. I tell him to hurry up but he pays no attention and so I order him out. He still doesn't budge. *I have to admit that a little bit of panic washes over me at this point, envisioning having to physically drag him out to the car, kicking and screaming.* But thankfully, after a couple of minutes he eventually gives in and makes his own way there to join the others, while I lock the front door.

"I think that *you'll* be having an early night tonight mister." I tell that back of his head with authority, as I follow him to the car.

"NO I WON'T!" He shouts back at me, without turning around as he marches towards the car.

"Oh yes you will, you're acting like a spoilt little brat and all over where you are going to sit on a five minute journey, for goodness sake." I continue, as I open the driver side door. "YOU ARE NOT A GOOD MOTHER TO ME! I WISH YOU WEREN'T EVEN IN MY FAMILY!!" He screams out so loud that I'm sure the entire neighbourhood could hear, before slamming the car door shut behind him and even I'm shocked. And at the very moment that this passes Johns lips, everyone inside the car knows that this time he has gone too far! Nobody dares to speak for the entire journey.

Mental note - To pay more attention to who sits in the front and when, or better still to have set days to avoid any guesswork (if nothing else, at least I will undoubtedly remember tomorrow)!

We walk to the boys individual classes in silence. Henrys classroom is the closest, then Lloyds and lastly Johns. As I leave the other two I kiss them both and cast them a cheeky smile, before mouthing 'I love you' as they set off, on their very best behaviour. Leaving just myself and John. When we reach his class he tries to hand me his bag, while he takes off his coat. *Not happening buster!* I glare at him and tell him to go inside. At which point he says, still obviously extremely cross with me by the look on his face "SORRY!" before disappearing, without a kiss nor backwards glance and I walk away, feeling unsure about how his day will pan out, being that it started so bad but decide not to pre-warn the teacher so as to give him the opportunity to redeem himself. In the past, this mood would usually be a 'no eye contact from the teacher when I collect him', kind of day but today is a work day for me and so I won't get to see them all now until after their clubs finish, at around five thirty tonight. *Which in all honesty, as bad as it sounds, today I am grateful for!*

Instead I look forward to the inevitable note in his contact book and an evening of lecturing him about remembering to have 'kind words' and 'kind hands' and all of the other jargon that they are taught in school, that we try to implicate at home too.

And upon collection at five thirty, I not surprised to find that I'm right... and so our lectures fill his entire evening.

Tuesday morning isn't that dissimilar from Monday. After going to bed apologising to me for being rude and telling me how much he loves me, John has woken up with the devil in him again. I try to tip toe around his mood, to save another row but when he won't let me do his hair it results in another pre-school argument between us. Thankfully not as bad as yesterday's incident and he goes into school looking like a street urchin, with his hair poking out at all angles.

Myself and his new teacher have a little thing going with John about his hair - we both tell him, that he acts more responsible and is kinder and happier when his hair is arranged spiking upwards and so when he's sad or mad he flattens it to down, which helps us judge his mood. *Well this morning will be case of being forewarned is forearmed, at least she will know instantly what kind of day she's going to have with him as he walks through the door!*

Lloyds friend Jack has come over for tea tonight and is currently nursing a bleeding nose with a cold compress, after a wrestling match that went horribly wrong. Initially John was jumping around the furniture pretending to be Dolly Parton and juggling with his invisible massive boobs, all the while laughing his head off and singing out 'Jolene, Jolene, Jolene Jo-lene'. *What must our neighbours think?!*

His character then transformed in 'John Cena' from WWE (whose well versed catch phrase *'You can't see me!'* in an American accent whilst having a hand waved across you face, can get quite annoying after the hundredth time of hearing it) and as he hurled himself off of the sofa in a 'slam dunk' action, he head butted poor Jack square on in the face, causing an instant scream of pain, followed by a gush of blood. *Luckily I had managed to get him into the kitchen before his hands began to over flow and spill onto the floor.*

I can now hear Lloyd shouting at John, while he stomps off sulkily to his bedroom screaming back at him that it was an accident and close behind follows Henry who, as usual is sticking up for Henry, much to Lloyds absolute disgust.

Mental note - To hide the wrestling DVD before he goes looking for it again and we have to endure hours and hours of fighting!

So that you can picture the scene, our front room is often home to a 'boy made' wrestling ring with our children, other people's children and more often than not Dick too, beating the life out of each other whilst counting down how long they have been pinned to the ground. These are the occasions that I actually quite enjoy (bizarrely), as they allow me the rare opportunity to slip away unnoticed and undisturbed for a full ten minutes before inevitably someone comes looking for me, usually screaming that they have been injured, followed by a detailed account of what rules had been agreed before the game had started and how the 'injurer' had flouted these rules. My response differs depending on how many times during the course of the game I had cause to yell out (in a robotic fashion) 'Someone's going to get hurt' and varies from loving Mother to 'Well it's your own fault, you shouldn't play so bloody rough, how many times did I warn you all that this would happen!'

Wednesday morning starts off much more promising, when Henry manages to dress himself *(all bar his socks)* for the first time ever. It took a while and he looks a bit twisted but he's so pleased with what he has managed to achieve that we all dance around, telling him what a big boy he is and he's loving the attention. I even find him a sticker from the cupboard, so that he can tell his teachers when he gets to school and he is elated.

This joy is short lived though when he then accidentally pours an entire bowl of porridge over himself and when I strip him off to redress him, he goes absolutely mad because he thinks that he will lose his sticker. I immediately peel it off and place temporarily on my own jumper reassuring him that I'll look after it, thinking that this will do the trick and keep him calm, but no, he desperately wants to put his new found talent of dressing himself into action again but as we are now running approximately ten minutes late I have to wrestle him to do it... so today it's his turn to kick off!

When we finally reach school, still in his little mood he refuses point blank to walk and instead sits in the middle of the footpath sulking, much to the amusement of every passerby; who smile at him and comment on how cute he looks, which just adds fuel to the fire. He flies off, into one of his rants and for the third time this week, I am happy to leave the school gates alone.

At this point in a bad week you usually think to yourself 'well, it can only get better'... but something's telling me that this won't be the case this week.

Mental note - To find a buyer for my children.

And I couldn't be more right! The post is pushed through the letterbox on Thursday morning by our chirpy, half dressed postman and sitting right on the top of the pile staring up at me as bold as brass, is a fine from a work trip to London I had made a few weeks previous. Instantly I remember something that I had neglected to remember since that journey and feel totally raged at myself!

I had forgotten to pay the bloody congestion charge and the photo evidence doesn't even allow me the pleasure of trying to contest it.

Then on Friday just to top the week off, I dent the car on the *(in my opinion)* over sized bollards in the Marks and Spencer's car park, whilst having a discussion on my mobile *(hands free of course)* with quite frankly a con artist that 'No, I haven't been in an accident lately, nor has any of my family and requesting very politely through gritted teeth, that he takes my details off of his database.

JUST as I hear the sound of metal being crushed and realise what I have just gone and done. *Ironic hey?!* Luckily for him, in the chaos of it all I had managed to cut him off, otherwise he might have been in for an ear bashing. So by the time that evening comes around I am extremely happy that at last, the weekend is here again and my plan is to do as little as is physically possible, to avoid any further bad luck. Curry night is its usual success, apart from the massive tip that the boys have mistakenly awarded the delivery guy *(but to be fair, some of the blame for this has to lie with us and our cowardliness)* . Afterwards, we snuggle down to watch one of our favourite shows 'Gogglebox', whilst consuming copious amounts of much needed wine. This programme is always guaranteed to lighten even the darkest of moods. We watch people in their homes, commenting on programmes and people that they see on their TV and we, in turn spend the entire programme relating these people to people we know. Always concluding that we most like are Stephanie and Dominic, the couple that drink far more than they should but deem it necessary and a vital ingredient to maintain our seemingly calm approach to parenting.

Saturday morning I awake, following a dream about swimming, to find that I am actually lying in a puddle of our own little calf-boy's recycled milk pee and so with a self induced head ache, I begin stripping the bed at 7am, any chance of a freakishly rare lie-in again just a fantasy.

By 8am everyone's hungry and so I start making breakfasts. Lloyd wants his standard 'BS' as he fondly refers to this weekend treat. *No, not a bullshit sandwich...* it's actually a bacon sandwich, cooked to perfection with no burnt bits, all of the fat cut off of the bacon and the crusts off of the bread with a thin scrapping of butter and no sauce. *Get this wrong and he'll moan his head off and refuse to eat it, leaving you wanting to rub his little nose in it!*

The other two have beans and cheese on toast and Dick has a fry-up using up whatever we have in the house to best resemble a 'No. 2' in the cafe . He then goes on to polish off any leftovers from the boys, who pass it along the table in his direction, whilst fondly saying 'Here you go Dusty Bin' and laughing, totally unaware of the character but fully understanding the humour and the underlying insult that they are being allowed to get away with. By the time I get around to preparing something for myself, I don't really fancy and so just have a bacon sandwich too.

Just as we start to tackle homework, Mum calls to let me know about an offer that she's seen on TV and wants to know when I'm next going to the shops because she wants to come along with me. I tell her that I'll call her back after we've finished, as I'm well aware that this could well be an hour's conversation but she doesn't hear me, because she hasn't come up for breath yet. *I swear that this is where Lloyd gets his ability to talk the hind legs off of a donkey from!* The only difference between them is that she can't pronounce most of the words that she says. 'Trifle' is 'triffel', 'Millennium' is 'Malidiem' and there are hundreds more! The funniest example was from the just the other day, when she pronounced 'Dyslectic' as 'Diclestic'... oh the irony! Me and Dad just looked at each other and wet ourselves laughing, whilst she was left wondering why and getting the hump slightly because she wasn't in on the joke, although knowing full well that it was about her.

Not only does she talk a lot, she also has a spending obsession. Dick says that she's got 'See it, buy it disease'. Half of her garage is taken up with her mini 'Shop', which is literally stacked like a mini market, with hundreds of tins, packets, boxes of sweets, jars of coffee.. you name it, she's got at least three of it We often joke that she could feed an army without popping out for reserves. A few years ago Dad suffered a brain injury and so doesn't drive anymore and so her reasoning for this mass food storage is that she needs it, just in case her and Dad 'can't get out'.

After the fourth "Yeah, okay then", she finally gets the gist. "Go on then, sod off, I'll speak to you later on." She says and so I hang up and go back to helping out with everyone's homework.

We eventually finish everything and go on to discuss our lottery numbers for this week. I have chosen: '5' as this is the number of sets of bed sheets I have washed this week. '7' The number of bad days I have had. '27' The age I would like to be again, as it was pre-children *(on hearing this explanation, all of the boys scour at me and tell me not to be so mean)* and '30' the total amount of socks I have put on between myself and Henry this week.

Dick chooses: '1' and '49'... *again!* I prompt him to try harder next week, otherwise he'll be thrown out of the game and won't share in our profits when we eventually win the jackpot! To which he points out that we have a joint bank account *(Mr Bloody-know-it-all)*.

Lloyd chooses: '2' as he has been allowed two Subways this week, making this the best week of his life so far *(for his gross combination of tuna, salami and cheese on warm bread, yuck)!* '4' As this is fast becoming his favourite number, his explanation 'because it's the two lowest even numbers added together' of course?! '6' The number of books that he has read this week and 8 to finish off the even number pattern that he has just realised he has created, much to his joy?!

John chooses: '6' his age.   '18' The age he wants to be. '38' my age *(I'm getting the feeling of déjà vu)* and '48' his highest score on Lloyds Twister tetras game - that he didn't ask permission to play and so this causes an instant argument, ending with Lloyd warning him that he will 'duff him up' if he goes in his bedroom and use his stuff again without asking.

We all know what number Henry chooses and the chaos that it inevitably brings!

So, with everyone happy and in agreement, this week's lottery numbers are as follows + one lucky dip:

Line One: 1, 5, 7, 27, 30 and 59.

Line Two: 2, 4, 6, 8, 18 and 48.

At this point the phone rings again and again it's Mum, calling to see if I 'forgot' to call her back.   I explain that that's not the case and that even though it is now 2pm, we have only just finished everyone's mountain of homework. But straight away, it's as though she's been on 'pause' since she hung up the last time and she quickly picks up where she left off and by the time that I put the phone down, I have somehow agreed to take her to the shops today, so that she doesn't miss out on the offer that she originally called about. Even though, I know in my head that most offers are on for at least a week, she has cleverly managed to convince me that the item will be sold out in a matter of hours because it's such a star buy!

I know, even as whilst I'm agreeing to take her on the phone, that in approximately an hour's time, when we finally locate them somewhere in the abyss of this shop, she will have managed to have filled the trolley so high that Dad will look like the cartoon character 'Chad', with just his eyes and nose visible above the piled high trolley.

And, that back at the car he and John will have bags under their feet, on their laps and even on top of their heads if there's no space left, whilst her lap will be bare as she angrily rants about why she has taken so long because obviously it wasn't due to the amount of shopping that she's done?!

Like the time that she was behind someone that paid all in coupons or another time where the till operators switched shift just as it got to her turn and then spent five minutes chatting before serving her

I manage to lose out of three children when I mention the word 'shopping' but John aka 'my shadow', wants to come along and, to be honest I don't mind because he's good company. He doesn't moan and he's actually very helpful. Not only that, he tends to get very grumpy if he stays indoors for long periods of time.

We leave the house, and although I'm no longer there I know exactly what's going to be happening - Dick will have plied Henry with a huge beaker full of hot shaky milk and put Peppa Pig on the TV through 'You Tube', so that it will stream for hours and hours meaning that he won't move. Thus enabling him and Lloyd to play on the XBox undisturbed, right up until the time we get home.

When we arrive at my Mum and Dad's house, they are of course not ready. So we sit in the car for five minutes. During this time, I dare John to sing loudly upon their arrival 'Why are we waiting, why are we waiting... for NANNA!' He takes on the challenge and excitedly sings away when they appear at the car but unfortunately Mum doesn't see the funny side at all and instead opens the door muttering, with a stern look on her face.

"Bloody cheek! It's not me that you've been waiting for, it's your Father. I told him you were coming straight down but he won't be rushed!"

Woops, I've got him into a row already!

"You don't mind if he comes along too do you?" She asks, still cross.

As if I would?!

"Of course I don't mind!" I reply, feeling immediately sorry for him and slightly annoyed that she has felt the need to check this with me. John idolises his Grandad and cuddles straight into him, whilst he updates him about everything and everything in between.

"He just wanted to get out for a walk". Mum continues, as she battles to untangle her handbag from the seatbelt. *He's always loved to walk and hated shopping and so he must be desperate! Mental note - We MUST take Dad out to the Country Park soon, while the weathers nice, he'd much prefer this type of outing, maybe we'll take Wilf their dog too.*

"I would have reserved it." She goes on, randomly changing the subject referring back to the sale item.

"But I just can't get up there to collect it. You don't mind taking me do you?" She checks again.

"Of course not." I say, whilst secretly wishing that I was lying on the sofa watching crap on the TV.

"I could have asked one of your sisters but I knew they were busy today." She continues and I smile to myself because I know that to wait even a day longer would have killed her!

"Just please, don't be all day!" I plead as we arrive at the shops, where inevitably I know that her 'speed shopping' is about to begin and she casts me a dirty look back.

"I don't need much" she says and, whilst me and John turn to raise a sarcastic eyebrow at each other, she's disappeared, with Dad as her wing man pushing the trolley behind her.

"As if she thinks we would fall for that!" I whisper to John laughing and he pulls one of his silly faces in agreement, making us both laugh again.

We stroll around the store and pick up what we need, we then go back out to wait in the car with an ice cream each and sit listening to some music while we wait for Mum and Dad finally emerge and when they do, we all pack up the car until it's fit to burst.

It's not until we are nearly back at their house that I realise that in all of this morning's mayhem, I forgot to register our lottery numbers and it's getting late.

"Oh bollocks!" I suddenly yell out loudly, giving everyone the fright of their lives.

"Oh my god, what?!" Screams Mum back at me in surprise.

"I've forgotten to do our lottery numbers." I say with a little less volume.

"Oh Jesus Christ, is that it?! Are you trying to give your Dad another bloody heart attack." She says firmly shaking her head. "There was a time that you didn't swear in front of me and ya Father you know!"

"Sorry." I reply, realising that I had maybe gone slightly over the top, but if I ever needed a week to win the lottery, this would be it!!

"God, it's not the end of the world! Why don't you stop off and buy them now? Have you got your numbers with you? " She asks matter-of-factly and I rummage around in my jeans pocket, lifting my bum off of the seat whilst trying to hold the steering wheel straight and can see her panic out of the corner of my eye - she's a nervous passenger at the best of times.

"Ah ha!" I yell.

"Hhhmmm, but I really do prefer to it online." I say, pleased to have found the scrap of paper that I wrote the numbers down but annoyed at myself for not remembering this morning... I NEVER forget!

"Well, they stop selling tickets in ten minutes, so you won't have time to wait until you get home." She rightly points out.

"True. You're right, I'll pop into the little shop near yours." I conclude, still cross at myself but at least I still have time to redeem myself.

As we pull up outside, Mum realises that she has forgotten something on her list and so enters too and is immediately lost in another, smaller scale 'speed shop' for a further ten minutes after I return to the car and upon her return, Dad and I express our complete shock at this ability she has as she warns us both to shut up otherwise she'll beat us both. Then we're on our way again.

Mental note - If I want to nip to the shop, always ensure that I've dropped Mum off first if I want to get home within a reasonable amount of time!

After three hours of food shopping and hanging around, John and I finally get home and are pleased to be there! I enter the house first and call out to the others to come and help us unload the car, but the only person to appear is Henry - Dick and Lloyd are, as predicted too engrossed in the XBox to hear our arrival. He greets me with far too quickly, with a half hearted 'something's wrong and you haven't been here' smile, followed by a massive cuddle. I prize his little arms from around my neck so that I can gage his facial expression and see what's wrong.

I soon realise that I'm wrong to do so though, because at that exact moment, he projectile pukes and it goes all over my face and even in my mouth! I try to disguise the fact that I am now heaving, whilst fighting back the sick that's pushing its way up my gullet and speak softly to Henry, in an attempt to calm him down because he is totally freaking out. Lloyd doesn't help the situation, he appears at the top of the stairs, looks down at the pair of us drenched in Henrys vomit and yells out at the top of his voice whilst pretending to reach. "EEEEEEERRRRRRRRR, THAT IS GROSS!!!!!!! Oh my god, I'm not going anywhere near it!!"

He then slowly and dramatically makes his way down the stairs, with his nose hidden under his t-shirt, in an attempt to mask the smell. At which point Dick bolts down the stairs too, like a young boy realising that he's in big trouble.   He says quickly, in a panicked tone as if thinking *'Oh shit!*   "He's been absolutely fine all the time you've been gone!"

"*Really?* Have you even looked in on him since I closed the bloody front door?" I question him, my sarcastic tone and volume saying it all, followed by a look to kill, sending him instantly into a 'better be the adult' mode and he scolds Lloyd for being so unsympathetic, before instructing him to go and fetch the *(lovingly named)* 'sick bowl' - which, I feel I must state is never used for any other purpose than this.

Dick then clears the sick up, whilst I strip Henry off and shower us both down and my thoughts are taken back to a post that I saw recently on a social media website, in which it showed a gravestone and on it was carved 'In loving memory of sleep, too suddenly taken from us by children'". How true! I'm under no illusions that tomorrow morning I will wake up, after only having intermittent sleep all night, feeling as though I've been beaten over the head with a sledge hammer!

All cleaned up, Henry and I retreat up to my bedroom where I lie out lots of old towels over the bed to catch the sick onslaught, that I know is imminent.

Sweet little John cannot do enough for either of us, he massages our feet, sings us songs and rubs Henrys face, all in an effort to make him feel better and to cheer me up. (He's so cute when he sings, he tries so hard to reach the notes that his little voice box goes all wobbly but you can't laugh at him or he will get all embarrassed and stop, believing that you're mocking him). Dick and Lloyd on the other hand, try to don this 'sympathetic' approach too but it's just irritating because it's not a natural instinct to either of them and so, to be 'helpful' they stay out of the way. Hidden downstairs I am fully aware that they secretly love the fact that they have been handed on a plate, the opportunity to watch 'boy' films for the rest of the evening without having to consider whether myself or the other two boys would enjoy them or not. *As usual, they have managed to have quite a nice day, whilst I've been running around like a headless chicken!!*
I then spend the rest of the evening and throughout the night rubbing poor Henrys back and clearing up a mixture of congealed milk-and-baked bean sick, all of the while thinking to myself 'tomorrow can only better!'

Mental Note - To disinfect the entire house tomorrow, so that it doesn't spread to anyone else... I DO NOT want a dose of this!!

3

Nothing ventured.. nothing gained!!

Sunday turns out to be a much better day, Henry and I remain in bed until early afternoon catching up on lost sleep and cuddling 'cuddles of reassurance', to let him know that he will soon feel better.   During the periods that he sleeps and I am unable to, I lay in bed staring up at the ceiling. The smell of disinfectant rife the air.   I run my fingers through my hair and they instantly get caught up in the tangles of crusty dried sick, from his hourly vomiting episodes throughout the night.   My body is too tired to move, let alone shower.   I can hear the mayhem going on downstairs, mainly being created by Dick, he isn't used to having to actually contribute to our morning routine, let alone be in charge of things. I turn over, chuckling smugly to myself and try to enjoy this rare opportunity of being horizontal and almost alone for as long as I can, before one of my other children finds me and interrupted the peace with their tale telling.

I run my own design company from home and from time to time find myself daydreaming, when business is slow or I have a particularly bad day, about changing my lifestyle *but* invariably life is always so hectic that my thoughts are usually interrupted, meaning that my routines continue unaltered and before I know it, another year has passed by with no change.

Today though, with no one daring to enter the 'quarantine zone' for fear of contracting 'the dreaded bug', I am allowed the unexpected pleasure of lying back and just pondering life for hours whilst listening to the chaos downstairs without having to get involved. *And it wasn't even me that's sick, how nice!* I have a list of 'job possibilities' that I have been mulling over for quite some time now. These include:

1. Going to work for someone else, doing my current job, so that I have less stress and won't have the hassle of never really being off duty... but I don't think that I could have someone else telling me what to do in my area of expertise - I'd probably want to smack them one straight in the mouth. So with that thought in mind, that's a 'no' *(I don't want to end up in prison for GBH)!*

2. A teacher... but what would I teach? Probably something design related. But, if I'm going to completely change my career, maybe I could do something totally different? I like computers too, so that's a possibility.. although surely I would need some actual technical knowledge of computers to be able to teach others, just liking using them won't be enough. So I suppose that's a 'no' too.

3. A PA... but what if I didn't like who I was a PA to? Also, I don't want to have to go to evening events, I rarely get to go out for my own social life let alone waste a babysitter on someone else's! And anyway, evenings for me are for being at home, cuddling my children... *and when they're in bed, drinking wine.* So that's also a definite 'no'!

4. Working in a shop... oh yeah, I used to LOVE working in shops when I was younger! Chatting to all of the regulars and the oldies, they'd update me on all of their gossip and then I'd get told off for talking too much. But I'd have to work weekends and over the Christmas period, something for which my children would never forgive me. So that one's also a definite 'no' too.

Hhhmmm... back to the drawing board! I have to start thinking outside of my usual 'favourites' list - maybe it's not just my career but my complete way of life that needs to change?
At which point I remember back to a book that Mercy lent me, it was about stripping down your past and present likes / dislikes / thoughts and dreams and creating a 'blueprint' of myself. I'll dig that out again.   I had started reading this book a while ago but could never get through a single chapter without being bothered for something by one of the members of my family
So now I start to consider my own 'blueprint'...
My life is one big drama. I like being creative. I like being in control. I like expressing myself. I like entertaining people. I like making people laugh. I am passionate and focused with everything I take on. I don't like to give up. I like studying people. I like to be heard. I'm bored if I'm not busy. I like to be there, should my children, family or friends need me. I like my magpies, I see them as spirits of people past (especially my Grandad) and feel comforted when I see them, which is ALL of the time. And I like wine *(I'm not sure whether this is relevant but it is definitely part of my blue print that can't be ignored).*

Mental note - To drink less wine!

I ponder on my blueprint for quite a while, trying to match it to a suitable job/lifestyle and then, from nowhere, SUDDENLY I HAVE A EURIKA MOMENT!   I could keep running my business AND write a book during the quiet periods... I could be a famous 'Author' and take on a whole new separate identity!   I don't know why this hasn't been on my list of jobs before?!

 The only catch is, being someone that neither reads a lot of books nor has ever wanted to write a book, I don't know where to begin *or* of course if I would be any good at it but, I decide that I'm going to give it a go anyway... after all nothing ventured, nothing gained!

4

That's it... I'm going to be a famous novelist!!

Now, where to start? I look around the kitchen for something to inspire me, for something to really get my juices flowing... but find absolutely nothing! So venture out into the garden to see whether I have better luck there. I stare out to the trees at the bottom... nothing. *Hhhmmm, this may be a bit more difficult than I had first anticipated!* After a while I'm joined by John, who inquires ever so sweetly..
"Mummy, are you having a breakdown?"
"No darling, I'm trying to find some inspiration. Mummy's going to write a book!" I state, trying to sound wise, with my eyes now transfixed on the trees, as though I have been hypnotised.
"Oh." He replies, less impressed than I would have liked. We stand in silence together for a full five minutes, me staring out at the trees and him staring at me, before he continues again with a scrunched up nose. "Let's go in yeah? It's pouring now, the neighbours might think that you're a bit erm... mad!"
He's right, I hadn't noticed just how wet and cold I am. It's June, last week was glorious sunshine for goodness sake, if this is climate change it can do one! I take a deep breath in and the cold air stings my throat.

My slippers are soaked through, my feet numb. I peel my eyes away from the trees and look down at his shivering little face, his lips are a slight shade of blue and he's wearing his usual attire of shorts and a t-shirt, that he wears regardless of the season. *I have a feeling that he might be a postman when he grows up.* And it's at this very moment that I realise something... I have a permanent and never ending source of inspiration for my writing, right at my fingertips.... my family!

Mental note - Try not to freak the kids out with weird behaviour! I don't fancy a visit from social services, trying to figure out whether I am insane... although at times I do feel that way.

Excited by my realisation I bend down and give him a cuddle before we both go indoors, where I throw my slippers into the washing machine and immediately begin my 'research' by bombarding my three kids with questions...

Question one - If I wrote a book and based a character on you, how would I best describe this character?

Lloyd *(who's just eight but could wrongly be mistaken as a 78 year old at times due to his mannerisms),* described a perfect child, well mannered, good at everything, especially technology and yet still totally "cool" and popular. Now, I'm not one of those parents that give their children false hope, so I told him that I would have to write him out of the story before I had even started because my imagination wouldn't stretch that far from the truth!
John who always displays the cutest expressions, with his wonky little grin, replied.
"Describe me however you like Mummy". I love you SOOO much!"

Aaahhh he sounds just the sweetest doesn't he? And he is don't get me wrong, but there have been many occasions over the past year that, if he were still small enough to fit, I would have happily poked him back up where he came from.. but we're over that phase now. *(PMA - If I say it enough times, it will be the truth)!*

The response from a very loud and squeaky Henry is simply: "Make me some shaky milk Mummy.. hot shaky milk!!!" In a high pitched, deafening tone (as standard).

By this he means warm strawberry milkshake, which he instantly knows that he isn't going to get, given the way he has requested it and so, after a long pause and with the sweetest smile growing slowly across his little face *(whilst I glared at him like an evil head mistress)*, he adds..

"P-l-e-a-s-e." As he hands me one of his many cow print beakers to re-fill for him.

All of my children are aware, even at this young age that are only two things that I cannot tolerate and that is rudeness and moaning. If I hear a child moaning *(and that extends to any, not just my own)*, I can actually feel the anger working its way up to the tip of my head, like an unexploded bomb. Luckily, my children are well aware of the tell-tale signs of this and the implications should I reach the explosion state, that they usually know when to stop pushing their luck and shut up. I'm sensing that in this instance 'The Look' *(as my children like to call it)* was enough to nip any whining in the bud.

Henry's at that age where he asks questions but then disagrees with the information you have supplied him with, arguing about anything and everything! He is very intelligent for his age, he counts beyond fifty, can write his own name, reads in excess of thirty of his friends and family's names and speaks exceptionally well.

However, during his increasingly frequent 'rants' he sometimes veers into his own language, where he has undoubtedly invented his own take on swear words, judging by the maddened look on his face, as he bellows at his brothers and on occasion me too, if he's feeling brave. Little does he know that this actually makes him look quite cute, with his little sticky-outy ears and reddened cheeks. What upsets him the most is that he considers himself as intelligent and as grown up as the older two, even though he fails to realise that he can't yet dress himself or wipe his own bum?!

His latest major rant, *much to the other two's absolute amusement*, is to swear blind when asked his age, that he is seven years old and gets quite irate when they laugh and ask him the question over and over again so that they can hear his response.   Which, more often than not results in him giving one or both of them a sly pinch or punch and inevitably ends in a full scale fight between them all.   I'll give him his dues, this kid has courage!   Most children would *not* mess with our middle child if they'd have seen him in action before, he can scare even the hardest of characters - but he gets away with it as the pair of them are best buddy's!
They share practically everything, including their room and often gang up on the eldest, who finds it impossible to get his head around how they have become so close and not include him *(the constant torment may be a slight clue)*.   So, even at three years old *(not seven)* he knows that he'll be forgiven, if he suggests playing 'Mums and Dads' and offers to be the baby, without arguing the toss.

Question two - What makes your character quirky?

Lloyd response is:
"Hhhhhmmm that fact that I'm a weirdo?   I LOVE chocolate.   My building skills are epic!   I'm the best person I know at Lego and Minecraft.   Oh and Maths".   *He's not one to wait in line to be praised.*   He then adds:

"Oh yeah, I nearly forgot about my Egyptian feet!"
This derives from a conversation that we had one evening
whilst watching TV, about my husband's odd shaped feet
and toe formation; he has a massive big toe on both feet,
with the smallest toe nail on each of these.   A family trait
apparently *(not one that is passed on to our children, I hope)*.   So we
spent the entire night looking up feet types on the internet
and his looked most like the 'Egyptian' style.   In case you
were interested, mine were 'Roman' and there was nothing
resembling my husband's shape funnily enough, they are just
too pre-historic!

John says:
 "My fighting abilities and my incredible weapons!   I could
chop the head off the biggest monster with my machete or
flattened the enemy with my shiny nun chucks".
He goes to school 'tooled up' with one of his ever increasing
collection of weapons on a daily basis - much to the obvious
disgust of some of the other parents. Most of these
weapons spend the majority of their life on top of one of the
kitchen cupboards, where they have been stored after being
confiscated because he has either hit someone or broken
something with them. *Oh god help me, I hope he gets through this
phase soon!*   Although even when John does get through it, I
am well aware that it won't be long until it's Henry's turn to
enter that phase because that's how it is in our house, like a
never ending tag team *('Groundhog day')*.   Yet given his
attraction to everything lethal, he is THE most loving child!
He strokes my hair every night and tells me that he loves me,
rubs my back when I'm sick, is sympathetic to everyone's
ailments and can read peoples expressions a mile off.
*Mental note - Try to steer him away from liking weapons.   Maybe I'll
buy him some books, teddies or something (anything) calmer and less
violent, he might calm down at school then too?!*
I dread school pickups, when the teacher sees me, but
pretends that she doesn't.   Avoiding all eye contact while I
wait my turn to eventually be greeted with...

"Can I have a word please?"   Followed by something like "I'm very disappointed to say that today your child has hit such and such or wouldn't do this or that..."
With this particular 'phase', first came the pushing, then the hitting and finally the biting.   For Lloyd it seemed to pass quite quickly but with John it is lasting what feels like a lifetime.   He hates school and is rebelling; which means that I seem to be telling him off all of the time and I hate it! Especially when I know that he has probably been told off all day at school too and will be scalded again by Dick in the evening, when he asks how the day has gone for him.   But... hopefully he's nearly over it now *(there's that PMA again)*.

Mental note - To let some things go, there are bigger things in this world to worry about and all kids go through bad spells at some point in their lives.   Hopefully this will mean that when he's in his teens, he'll be an angel!   PMA!!

Henry's response again is milk orientated, he says..
 "I LOVE shaky milk.   Hot shaky milk!   Can you make me some shaky milk now please?"
This is SO true, he does love milk!   Every five minutes, from the minute his eyes open until he's snoring in his bed, he is asking for the stuff... repeatedly over and over again and if you're not fast enough, he's in the fridge, lid off of the milk, milk spilt everywhere with the microwave door open at the ready.   At this point, he will have also turned the fridge up, meaning that in a few hours, when you open the fridge door again, everything will be frozen *(the amount of soggy cucumbers and stiff strawberry's that have been thrown away in our house is unbelievable)!*

He's out of nappies during the day now but his night nappies are SO full of bloody pee because of the copious amounts of milk consumed, that I am continuously washing bed sheets, where it has over-flown and leaked out of the sides and the little calf-boy has managed to sit on as many of our beds as is physically possible before it is removed. Subsequently there is usually a mountain of washing to do and all before 8am.

John then points out that another thing that makes Henry quirky, is that he is ALWAYS naked and he's right about that too, he never has any clothes on! Within two minutes of walking through the front door, you can guarantee that he has stripped off and his clothing maps out a trail of where he's been. His nakedness is so normal to the rest of us, that sometimes we open the door to the postman or other complete strangers and wonder why they are looking slightly uncomfortable, only to look down and see a naked Henry bending over to show them his bum crack or on other occasions, pulling at his willy saying "Look, fat peanuts!" He's got this pleasant little saying from Lloyd, who, following a sex education class at school decided to educate the others two. John also learnt that.. "Men have peanuts and women have chinas." *(I mean, what do you do hey)?!*

Mental note - I should possibly run through a quick and very basic educational sex talk with them all at some point, so that they have their facts right before one of the school Mum's collar me and I have to answer questions about inappropriate conversations.

Dick has also provided me with quite a lot of ammunition for his character over the years too, by doing some *really* stupid things! Like walking into the patio doors at high speed with a beer in his hand and nearly knocking himself out.

Or asking, whilst on holiday in Margarita what his name translated to, only to be informed that it is actually 'Shitty Penis', much to the amusement of absolutely every native there! Calls would be heard over the sound system saying things like

'Hey, shitty penis could you come to the bar' *or* 'Look everybody, Shitty Penis is in the pool.

This was something that happened approximately fifteen years ago but still causes me to literally laugh out loud on a regular basis when I think back or to the other extreme, when he has really annoyed me, I find myself mumbling it offensively under my breath, as if to really going to offend him *(it never works though)*.

On breaking the news to other people, I had mixed reactions. My sisters and Dad were supportive and offered to read my work as I went along. My Mum on the other hand, was very concerned that I may write a book about her and portray her in a bad way, which I thought was slightly vain! So I wound her up by telling her she was the focus of the book and that I was going to call her 'Pat' as in 'Pat Butcher' from EastEnders. She didn't find this very amusing and went on to tell me how annoyed she would be if I was mean about her in any way! *Me... as if?!*

My friends loved the idea and we spent many occasion discussing over dinner or drinks what each of their characters names could be. *Something that I found hilarious!* I never before realised the power of a name or how we attach certain characteristics to certain names without realising it. Much to my surprise, I found that some people felt more accepted by people if their names are shortened or if they were called by their nick names and some people really hated their names.

These people described to me how they had spent their lives proving that they aren't boring, or mad, or a weirdo and all because of the name they were given at birth by their loving parents. Some of the suggested replacement names were SO unlike their current names and personalities that we would be in tears of laughter imaging how they could have turned out if they had been called this or that!

The next day I sheepishly bring the idea up with Dick, who nearly spits out his dinner in amusement. "Sorry... you're going to write a book? This isn't another money making scheme is it?" He says whilst laughing his head off.

"What's so funny?" I ask, slightly pissed off by his reaction.

"Eva, you don't read. You run a company. You have three children to look after. You are *forever* moaning that you have no time to yourself, that when you're not doing the washing or cleaning you're wiping arses or something equally as unglamorous! I thought you were trying to find more time for yourself, not stretch yourself further? When exactly are you going to fit it in, with all of the other dramas that occur in your life on a daily basis?!" He says, his words slipping off of his tongue a little too easily for my liking.

"When I'm not busy." I say quietly, still irritated although I try not to let him see this.

"Oh okay. I look forward to reading it then. Probably around the same time as when the boys leave home then." He says, still chuckling to himself while he flicks through his e-mails on his phone.

"You just watch this space, I'll show you." I warn him with narrowing eyes but he carries on with his sarcasm none the less.

"Hhhhhmmmm okay. Will it be like the job-lot of baby clothes that you brought, which are incidentally still sitting in the back of the van outside. Or the fancy 'high-end' animal beds, that you were going to make to sell to the rich and famous. Where's the wood for that? Oh yeah, still in the garage."

"Oh piss off!" I say sulkily, as I walk out of the room swearing about him in my head as I go. *Right, now you've done it... you bastard.* I'm going to prove you wrong!

My kids were really excited about the fact that I was writing a book too. They desperately wanted to be included in the storylines and wanted lots of input to their characters, even drawing pictures of themselves that they had hoped would be included. However, during a recent 'meet and greet' with Lloyds teacher, where I noticed that there were sheets of paper hanging around the class detailing how a story should be written, I asked excitedly and rather too loudly...

"Have you told your teacher that Mummy's writing a book?" To which he simply replied 'No', with a scrunched up nose, suggesting that he has just been humouring me with his excitement and so I'm guessing that this is the case with the other two too. *A bit rude!* So, from this point onwards I decide that initially I will keep my research 'underground', especially from Dick. Just until I figure out whether I'm any good at this writing malarkey, in the hope that this will save my idea being added onto my ever increasing list of 'money making schemes' as he likes to put it and give him another excuse to ridicule me!

I'm really happy that over the following weeks, people stop asking me how my writing is going as they forget about my big announcement, I thank god that I don't have to lie to everyone anymore *(just to my closest family and they will forgive me if I'm ever published)!*

In secret I begin to rack my brains, trying desperately to come up with storylines and characters and one night I decide that I need to alter my 'researching' method. I change my habits as much as I can, without it being too obvious so as to be caught.

On the weekends I suggest visits to places that wouldn't normally interest me.   During the week I nip out more often, sometimes late at night, using the excuse that I need something urgently, like milk or vegetables or that I've forgotten something - just to see whether I can bump into some 'odd people *or* if I catch people up to things that they shouldn't be *or* better still, with people they shouldn't be with.

The new approach proves a success and I'm feeling pretty good with myself for maintaining the secret, until nearly five weeks in, when I get a sense that Dick is becoming suspicious when he starts by asking lots of questions about where I had been and who I've seen.   He then starts questioning the boys about my behaviour too; who once probed, start making mental notes to leak back to him about my ever increasing disappearing acts, they even begin requesting to tag along when I say that I'm going out.

So I decided to restrict all 'spying' activities to during the day, whilst alone and within a few days life resumes back to normal again.

Mental Note - To try to be more discrete!

5

'Listen' contains the same letters as the word 'silent'.

Since my eureka moment, I have noticed a definite shift in myself. I have become more sensitive to other peoples body language. I find myself listening to their conversations and making notes on the way that they speak and describe things. I have realised that this is all part of their own personal 'blueprints' and weirdly, this has made me much more confident. I have always been fairly confident anyway but this is a different confidence, like I have an insider's knowledge because I am studying the subject of 'human beings', like I'm a secret agent gather evidence on people. I don't tend to feel the need to speak whilst around strangers when there are awkward silences anymore either. Instead of being the loud one that says the most inappropriate things at inappropriate times, I hold back and study other people's behaviour whilst trying to make my body language look like that of a very confident person. I've found that this planning, allows me time to think, before opening my big mouth.

This morning's start is similar to most, Lloyd gets out of the bath and 'helps gravity along' *(his words)* by swirling the water clockwise down the plug hole an even amount of times.

He's convinced that this empties the bath faster and this morning I don't even humour him by commenting on his weird behaviour.   Instead, as I run the next persons bath and add the bubbles, I try explaining to the boys what rhyming slang is, following a comment on TV last night, that they have picked up again this morning.

"For instance"   I start, prematurely pleased with myself about the link that I am about to make.

"Are you having a bubble bath?   Means, are you having a laugh?   Bath and laugh, rhyme."

"And, I'll bring the dust bin lids.   Means, I'll bring my kids. Lids and kids rhyme." I continue, still pleased with myself but now because I am remembering the phrases with such ease.

I then throw into the mix 'Apples and pears' and some other well know sayings. *All clean I promise.*   But they just can't get their heads around what I'm trying to explain and just stare at me confused.   Then John asks innocently.

"Do you mean like how Nana speaks?"   To which I crack up laughing, *even though I know I shouldn't!*

"No, she just gets a bit confused sometimes, she's always been the same bless her!"   I compose myself and explain sensibly while ushering him into the water to avoid running late.

"The people who say these types of sentences', do it on purpose."   I say and am about to continue when John interrupts me, looking totally confused and unimpressed.

"Oh right.   Why?   Don't people just think they're a bit, well you know."   He pauses and then gives me one of his silly faces as if to describe the word 'mad'.   Okay, he's right.   It is a bit weird when you think of it in detail and even I'm not interested in what I'm saying now.

"No, people just except it as the way they are.   Sometimes you start saying things in certain way and then just kind of carry on saying them for the rest of your life, without noticing that you are."

"Oh right." He says, still not convinced as he rubs the shampoo into his hair and some of the suds drip down into his eyes.

I hand him a towel and place Henry in the water beside him and at this point, I realise that not only was this was a crap conversation to start with, my explanations have also been crap and so promptly change the subject. But then spent the entire day racking my brains, trying to think of someone that we know who I could have used as an example. As I start thinking about friends and family, I find myself scribbling lists upon lists of words to describe each of them and before I know it, I have nearly filled an entire book with everyone's individual 'blueprints'. Some are long lists and some are short but as I read each, they make me realise why I like them all so much.

Mental note - To hide the 'Blueprint book, in case anyone else reads it and is offended by theirs, as I have since found that these lists are an ongoing - I quite often see someone doing or saying things and just have to jot it down before I forget, like a weird obsession.

Today, my other sister and brother-in-law Patsy and Greg have come over with their two girls, Grace and Lilly-Mae who are just beautiful. Greg loves his sport and so him and Dick immediately disappear off into the front room to watch the footy and drink beer, whilst managing to do something that only men can do, totally block out the children. Dick isn't a great football fan and so tries to keep up with the conversation but you can see that he's struggling from time to time with the detail. *Even though he had spent ten minutes swatting up the latest scores before they arrived.*

Patsy's work requires a lot of organisational skills with regards to other people, events, dates etc. and we often joke that she must use her full quota up during her working hours, as this is something that she lacks in her personal life.

More often than not a visit begins with her dropping her family members off first, whilst she returns home to collect some forgotten items to which we all laugh at the irony (this have included presents, cards, food etc.). She's the only one out us sisters that actively enjoys physical exercise and spends hours putting herself through her paces at fitness clubs, swimming and yoga, finished off with some art classes. I often make the promise *(that we all know will inevitably be broken)* to join her one day but I just have no coordination and unless it's swimming, walking or running am NO good at sports and I can never find the time to do any of the ones that I do enjoy. I am SO bad that Dick won't even play something as simple as table tennis with me anymore because he spends all of his time running after the balls, whilst I'm on the ground howling with laughter trying desperately not to wet myself. Even a simple game of Frisbee leads to him becoming irate, swearing that he'll never play with me again and lecturing the boys about how they had should make an effort to be better at sports than me otherwise no-one will want them on their team.

Our kids absolutely idolise each other! They are so relaxed in each other's company that when they are together, you would think they were brothers and sisters. On seeing each other, they instantly scream with excitement and spend the next half an hour at least, talking at such high volume that you feel as though you want to beat them with a stick to shut them all up. *Although you can't help but love seeing them all so happy and natural together.*

Grace is 11 going on 18 and everyone says that she reminds them of me, when I was younger *(the lucky devil)!* She hates pink, dresses as a Goth and has a quite grown up view on life for her age. Her witty little sense of humour is comical and she does *not* like any suggestion of being 'girly', instead she relishes in the idea of being a tomboy.

Lilly-Mae on the other hand is the complete opposite.   She looks like Patsy when she was a girl and has a sweet little smile that could allow her to get away with just about anything.   She's very girlie, loves everything pink and ADORES baby's.   She especially loves Henry because he has always been her 'real life baby'.   Henry was born very prematurely, at just under 27 weeks and so some of the little outfits that he wore in the first few months of his life are Lilly-Mae's baby's clothing, which makes their bond even tighter.   You can often hear her telling him how tiny he used to be and showing him how his old baby-grows look now on her dolls.

Within moments of being together she is pretending to be Henrys 'Mummy', pushing him around in a toy pram with a pink blanket over him and in the other room Lloyd and Grace link up their iPads to play Minecraft together, their separate worlds *(that they have spent untold hours individually creating)*, becoming one big world that they can communicate with each other in.. something I wasn't aware was even possible!?   They are instantly fixated, meaning that unless you offer them sweets or suggest a sleepover there is no way that you could penetrate their brains, even the cry of 'It's the end of the world', wouldn't filter through and there's conversations like..

"Have you seen the new update?"
"Oh yeah I hate it, do you?   I really don't like the way it makes you see things from above now."
"Oh god, no me neither."
"Do you think you can go back to the old version?"
"What's better diamonds or gold?"

Mental note - To educate myself in how they link their iPads and set up some parental guidance too, as I have NO idea what they are doing on them.   What a bad Mother I am!

After a few hours of constant noise, it's just too much to bear and so I suggest that they sit up at the table and do some drawing whilst I prepare dinner.   As I am now a fully fledged member of studying 'human beings' I stretch my 'blueprint' idea out to their minds too, asking them all to draw pictures of people that they know, either friends or family and pick out some features to highlight what they like / dislike about the people, so that they can see what makes them 'them'.   It all starts off quite pleasant, whilst scribbling away they discuss what they'd been up to at school, who had been in trouble, who had been rewarded for being good etc. Lloyd really looks up to Grace, he loves listening to all of her gossip from school.   She in turn, revels in being the oldest and considers herself to be the wisest and out of them all, only Lloyd challenges this by trying to outwit her.

Today she is trying to educate him and the others in the art of 'relationships'.   From time to time, me and Patsy listen in to their conversation in the kitchen and giggle at some of the topics covered.   Having three 'boy' cousins is quite a handy research tool for her too from time to time, as it means that she can get some male perspective and feedback on situations.   Lloyd opens the 'relationship' conversation by asking after one of Grace's friends, whom is someone that he neither knows nor has ever met.

"So, who's Gemma going out with now?"   He asks with obvious interest.

"You know she was with Robert right?"   She says whilst still drawing.

"Yeah."   He agrees, although he actually doesn't know him at all.

"Well, he wouldn't kiss her and so she dumped him.   She's now with Zachary because he told her that he'd kiss her at the school disco on Friday."   She updates him at speed.

"Is everyone allowed to watch?"   Lloyd asks.   *Weird question?!*

"Oh yeah!" She says and I'm not convinced that this topic has ever been raised but more that she's humouring Lloyd to add to the story's effect.

"They're going to do it just before the end of the night, by the toilets, so that anyone who wants to see can come and watch." She continues dramatically. *Really?*

"Timmy at my school kissed Ruby outside in the playground the other day and we all watched but then he got sent to the office coz one of the lunchtime leaders saw. You're not allowed to kiss in school time apparently." He informed her. *How did I not know about this?*

"Really?!" She exclaims looking up from her drawing, her eye's now glowing with gossip excitement.

"Oh, oh and Samuel yeah, well he dumped Rosie because he said that she moaned too much. He's right you know, she does moan a lot!" She says rolling her eyes.

"I thought they were going to get married?" More total strangers but Lloyd speaks again as though he knows these people well.

"Yeah I know, I couldn't believe it! Rosie cried for like, a week. She was SO upset! But now she's going out with Richie." She pauses to add to the effect.

"And Samuel is well jell!"

John also loves this type of conversation, although he doesn't like to admit that he likes this species of human being, with the exception of his family members *(I love his diplomacy)* he has an ever increasing amount of 'girl' admirers and so this offers a good insight.

And so the conversation continues for the next half an hour, leaving myself and Patsy feeling quite boring! The very mention of girls in this context, would embarrass and annoy Lloyd if I were to bring it up but he listens eagerly as Grace continues, his eyes full of admiration at how grown up she is.

In hindsight, I think I may have damaged Lloyd slightly by telling him not to get involved with girls too early on in life because girls can break your heart and wreck your life.... and that if this were to ever happen, I might have to physically hurt them.

Mental note - To take time to explain to the boys that having girlfriends isn't that bad and that I wouldn't be mad if they wanted to have a relationship.   And of course, I wouldn't actually floor any little girls at the school gates... well, not unless they were particularly nasty to any of them.

The conversation then moves on to their pictures and who they have drawn.   Grace holds up her picture confidentially and announces.
"This is Ted!"
Ted has swept back black hair, a football under his right arm and is apparently wearing the 'coolest' clothes and is the most popular boy in school... which of course, is why she likes him and is going out with him... and why all of her girlfriends are envious!   Lloyd has drawn me, with a piny on, cooking.   He's got the picture spot on actually, I am wearing trousers a jumper and have my hair back.. the usual attire and there's a sign above my head, which I read it aloud:
"Mum's the best cock ever!"
Ah bless him!   I know that that was meant as a compliment and not an insult, him and his bloody spellings!   Patsy and I fall about laughing but when I look down up at him, I try desperately to stop because I can see that his cheeks are pink with embarrassment and that he's upset.   At this point Grace also can't help but laugh too and this sends him over the edge, he flies into a rage, screws his picture up and stomps out of the room whilst John calls after him sarcastically.
"Oh alright, sweaty pants."
Following which Lloyds instantly reappears and is steaming! He attacks John like a boy possessed and I have to separate the pair of them.

I calm the situation down and we move onto Johns picture and once again I know that no insult is intended... but he has drawn Dick with a massive tummy, stubble, grey hair and has written 'Moobs' next to his *(frankly bizarre looking)* oversized nipples, which he describes as being the 'the pointy things, that feed baby's' and I try to explain that Daddy's can't actually breast feed, which is obviously too confusing for him to understand. I must say that Dick will be impressed though, at the rather large size of the 'peanut' that John has given him! He then goes on to tell us all how Aunty-M's 'boobies' are the biggest he has ever seen and again we are in fits of laughter. Henry didn't actually draw a person, instead he reverted to type and called the register throughout, with the kids all responding when requested to do so, that they were present.

Next up is Lilly-Mae, she has drawn Henry. He has a little body, little arms and legs and absolutely massive ears, that she affectionately explains this as being 'the cutest part of him'. I'm sure in years to come him may give her a dead arm for this portrait but in all of their innocence, he accepts the drawing followed by a massive cuddle and is chuffed to again be the centre of her attention. Next to him in the picture is her long suffering dog 'Scruff', in a pram. The poor little thing is so used to being dressed in baby clothing, that it doesn't know what it's supposed to be! During her explanation of the picture, she asks us all.

"Doesn't he just look SO sweet and fluffy?" To which we all agree *(although we all feel slightly secretly sorry for the real life Scruff)*.

When they leave, the house feels almost silent with the boys obviously disappointed that the girls couldn't stay over being as it's a school night and so I suggest snuggling under the duvet and watching the episode of Dr. Who that we'd missed on the weekend and instantly their moods are lifted from sombre to excited again, as they climb into their places.

Henry sits next to me and the boys on the single seats at the other end of the room, closer to the TV. They then take it in turns to move next to me for a cuddle before going up to bed, Henry first and then John and lastly Lloyd before I can sit alone, which is usually when the cat appears for her cuddle.

The next day I decide to go out and 'people watch' as research for my novel, whilst the boys are all at school. I take the half an hour drive to our biggest local shopping centre, park up in the frankly enormous car park, trying hard to think of something to remind me later of where to locate my car. I then take up position in a small little coffee shop on a corner, near the entrance, with a pot of tea, a slice of chocolate cake with my note book open and pen poised to jot down my findings. As I sat there, I think of something I heard on the radio the other day 'the word listen contains the same letters as the word silent'. So, I remain silent as I try to listen in to other peoples conversations. I study their body language and again, I feel like a secret agent.

On the table next to me, there are two elderly ladies and so I decide to begin with them. One appears quite hardnosed looking, whilst the another seams much to have a much softer face and both are of a similar age. My theory on this pair, is that they have always been good friends, their partners have now passed away and so they spend most of their time together, with the bossy one *(who looks like a 'Maud'),* taking on the role as an overpowering wife, whilst the sweet one *(who looks like a bit of a 'Madge'),* has taken on the role of the down-trodden husband. I imagine that every now and again, Madge just desperately longs to jump up and down like an idiot, shouting things like 'poo', 'bum', 'willy' to rebel but wouldn't dare to. I zone in...

"D'you know what, I can't believe the bloody cost of things now days can you? Bleeding extortionate!" Maud rants, as chews on a Belgium bun and then sips her tea to wash it down.

"I know." Replies Madge sipping her tea, not looking up from the table looking like a kicked puppy.

"I don't know how this generation can afford anything?!" Maud starts again, as angry about this as she was the last time she spoke.

"Oh I know." Answers Madge again, her eyes still not leaving the table.

"And, if they think they've got it bad, they want to try being a pensioner!" Maud continues with her rant, before wiping her mouth free of crumbs and asking.

"Where do you want to go next?"

"Erm.." The sweeter lady attempts to answer as she places her cup on the saucer but is rudely interrupted before she can finish what she was about to say.

"Drink up! Alice over the road said that Marks has got a sale on. We'll we go there, yeah?" She practically orders her and then gets up and toddles off, leaving Madge still seated with half a cup of tea left in her cup.

"If you like." The sweet old lady answers dutifully to the her back, as she puts her cup back down onto the saucer and rushes to follow after. *Ah, poor Madge, she should ditch Maud and find a new friend!*

Next up are a couple in their late teens, both very good looking with dark hair and bronzed skin. The girl is wearing tight jeans and a skimpy top, her finger and toes nails are manicured and her hair perfect. He too has skinny jeans on with a black designer t-shirt. His hair is very 'hip' all floppy and natural and the girl keeps running her finger through it affectionately. They are all over each other and I feel slightly uneasy at ear-wigging on their conversation in case I hear something that I shouldn't but decide to anyway. Who cares, I can't imagine that my life will *ever* be this romantic again!

"Are you staying at mine tonight?" The boy as he strokes her back. This one's definitely a 'George'.

"Well I don't know, Mum thinks that I should spend some more time at home." She says rolling her eyes as she continues.

"Her and Dad keep banging on about how I need to be more sociable with them and that they weren't born with the sole purpose of washing my clothes and cleaning up after me. They never see me anymore." She looks like an Ophelia to me.

"Oh come on babe." He pleads and kisses her check to try to pursued her.

"And then they wonder why I'm never there, do'ya know what I mean? Nag, nag, nag!" She continues, ignoring him.

"Oh come on baby.. stay." This time it's his time to ignore her, as he carries on with his pleading.

"Will your Mum mind if I stay again though, I feel a bit bad?" Ah and as easily as that, she's sold.. *well she didn't take much convincing did it!?!*

"Who cares if she does?!?" He says and the pauses.

"And anyway, if she has a problem with it, I'll just sneak you in and hide you under my covers and we can stay there, locked in my room all night."

I can't see his facial expressions at this point, as I'm way too embarrassed to look over at them in case they realise that I've been listening in this whole time but can imagine that he's looking at her with his best 'come-to-bed' eyes and a cheeky smile.

"Oh I don't know babe." Ophelia says unconvincingly.

Yeah right, who are you trying to kid!

"Oh come on baby! I'll do that thing again, you know with the little ..."

Oh bugger and ball bags!!!!! Out of my mouth comes the loudest screech as I watch my cake, as if in slow motion, plop directly into my tea cup. Luckily for me, I've been sitting there for quite a while now so the contents of my cup is almost cold but I can feel my face reddening, due to my way too loud outburst.

I slowly look around to find that all eyes are fixed on me and so decide that it is the time to leave the coffee shop and to give up the 'people watching' for the day. As I depart I scald myself for being such a klutz, *although in all honesty I'm more annoyed that I interrupted the couples conversation just as it was getting juicy!*

Mental note - To try to be more inconspicuous when under cover. Better luck next time!

I look at my watch and realise that I have actually been sat here for bloody ages and am now going to be late to pick the kids up from school *(doesn't time fly when you're being nosey).* In my rush to leave, I notice that the location of the tea stain makes it look as though I have wet myself and so use my bag to cover it. *Great, I've got to walk to the car like this and won't even have time to go home and change them either!?*

On the way home though, I see lots of magpies and so am perked back up at the thought that this may bring me luck this week... *maybe with the lottery?!* So the following morning and with this in mind, I am the first to choose my lottery numbers for this week's draw, which are: '9' The amount of times I have been vomited over this week. '15' the amount of magpies I spotted on my 'people watching' journey home and '44' because this will be how old Dick will turn on his next Birthday, which is in just a few weeks and I wanted to remind him of this.

Dick chooses: '5' His reason being that this is the age that I act the majority of the time *(oh touchy, was it something I said).* '1' and '49'... *honestly!?!* At this point, he rightly points out that he has added a number and so can't be ejected from the game.

Lloyd picks: '18' As this is the age he has decided that he wants to start working for Lego, creating scenes. '24' The age he wants to become an Inventor and '36' the age he wants to become a Scientist. So, all career related for him this week then.

John chooses: '6' His age and '18' the age he wants to be *(I'm seriously thinking of giving him the same warning as Dick if he doesn't buck his ideas on his choices soon)*, and '159' because this is how much ammo he has for his guns. I explain that it only goes up to 59 and so we decide on '01' and '59' instead, so as to still incorporate the same numbers.

I'm picking my rows this week and so have decided to bypass Henry, to save my eardrums but of course include '7' in our final selection as I know that this would be his choice. So, with everyone happy and in agreement, this week's lottery numbers are as follows + one lucky dip:

Line One: 1, 5, 6, 7, 9 and 18.

Line Two: 1, 18, 24, 36, 44 and 59.

But alas, after the big build up and the usual outcome, we don't win anything and are as usual all slightly disillusioned once again. This is soon forgotten though, as we enter into a few competitions via text and dream about how we will enjoy the holiday and car prize when we win it and later, when Lloyd launches into one of his never ending conversations, I point out that the holiday is for four people and that he will be the one that's left behind, so that everyone else can enjoy some peace and quiet to, just shut him up. It has the desired effect and he buttons it.

6

I knew he was a pervert!

It's Monday morning and after dropping the boys off to school in the usual hurried way, I drive to Mum and Dad's to give them a lift to a friend's house.   When I arrive, as standard they're not ready, their pace of life the total opposite of my own.

"We're just having our breakfast, do you mind coming in for a cuppa tea before we go, we won't be long?" Smiles Dad. *How can I argue with that face?!* Even as a more mature man of nearly 80 *(or an 'elderly' as Lloyd calls older people)*, Dad is still strikingly attractive with young features and kind eyes.

There are only a handful of people that I have ever known him to dislike and he is very positive and upbeat about life in general.   Everywhere he goes, people go out of their way to speak to him and everyone he meets comments about what a lovely man he is.   *Basically, there's nothing to dislike about him, he's just lovely!*

My Mum is a strong women with a big heart, who would give you her last pound if she could.   She is very much the boss of the house and used to run a her own business too but rather than slowing down in retirement, when me and Patsy had children she gained a new job... of becoming our very own unpaid 'Nanny'.   A job that they have both loved and were brilliant at too!

It's lovely because as the kids have grown up so closely with Mum and Dad, they idolise them *(the little sods also know exactly how to twist them around their fingers, as so get away with a LOT more than we used to)!* I have untold amounts of photos, sent to me by my Mum over the years showing each of the boys during their visits to their house, just to let me know that they are copping fine without me. That feeling of trust and unconditional love, just can't be brought and is very reassuring for an working Mother.

I decide to have some breakfast with them, as I don't feel that I have got to spend a decent amount of time with them for ages, which is a shame. Not only that, I'm going to the coffee shop again this morning for some more 'spy action', somewhere that I'm not keen on eating after the last time. As I sit at the table I feel guilty for not being able to tell Mum where I'm going because she'd love to come but I know that if she did she would be sure to blow my cover, she's rubbish at covering up the truth! And so I spend the entire meal trying to avoid the subject of what I'm up to for the rest of the day. Not only that, if she did come she wouldn't only just want to shop, she'd want to get involved too and she can create a scenario about just everyone and everything! For example, if we're travelling along the motorway and see an ambulance, she'll say something along the lines of 'Oh god, there's been an accident! I bet it's a bloody lorry driver, driving like he owns the road! Probably in the fast lane, they're not allowed to do that you know! I hope nobody's died.... for goodness sake, we'll be queuing on here for bloody hours now! This is why I don't like coming on the motorway!'

Mental note: To spend either Saturday or Sunday with the pair of them, the boys will love it and we can have a proper catch up... think I'll tell Mum what I'm up to then, I can't keep a secret from her for long!

Half an hour later Mum and Dad are *finally* ready to leave the house.   Mum gets into the car, just as I move the booster seat for her to sit down.   I flick a few manky old chips and some gummy bears away and make an effort in vain, to wipe the seat clean for her but she catches me and moans anyway. "Good god, this car is a bloody state!   Next time I'm bringing a towel to sit on!   Your Dads car was never like this, was it love?"

"No dear."   Comes the reply from the backseat, as he hands her the front door key for her to put into her handbag.

"Nor's Mercy's.   Hers is spotless, isn't it love?"   She continues.

"Yes dear."   He repeats again and I smirk to myself as I sense a hint of sarcasm in his tone.

"Okay, okay I'll get it cleaned, I just never get the time and anyway it's a waste of money, the boys don't look after it."   I defend myself.

"Well you're the grown up, it's up to you to teach them! This isn't exactly setting a good example is it."   She says looking around her in disgust.   *Oh whatever!*

Mental note - To get the car cleaned before I pick Mum up again next time and she is right,, it is absolutely disgusting!!

I drop the pair off, wave goodbye and make my way to the shopping centre wondering what and who I will encounter today, just as Suzanne Vega's 'Tom's diner' starts playing on the radio.   I turn it up, I love this oldie!!   I sing out loudly. *"Da, da, da, da, da, da, da, da, da, da, da, da, da, da ,da... it is always nice to see you, says the man behind the counter...."*
When I get there, I park up in the gigantic car park and make my way excitedly to the coffee shop, making a mental note of where I have parked (I don't want to make that mistake again, once it took me over a hour to locate it, with lots of bags, I was *not* a happy bunny)!   However on entering, I come down from my cloud slightly as I realise that the waitress from last week is on duty again.

She won't remember me, I reassure myself as I take a seat in the same spot as before and start to browse the menu. *I am SO wrong!* Instead, she greets me as if I were a close friend. "Oh my god hello! How embarrassing was last week!? Did you get the stain off of your bum?" She asks with obvious amusement.

Bum? The tea stain was at the front of my trousers and I thought that I covered it up well. What the hell is she going on about? She must have me confused with someone else that's had an equally embarrassing experience.

"It totally looked like you'd shit yourself! Did you see that young couple sniggering at you when you walked off? I really felt for you!" She continues, at such a high volume that people were starting to listen in and smile to themselves but I'm still confused.

"I have to be honest, it made me chuckle all day! I bet you were mortified!"

No... I am now though! 'Go away, you annoying women!!' I yell inside my head but she doesn't. Instead she carries on, telling me all about other sights that she has witnessed and how such events make for fantastic dinner party chat. *Great, so now I'm the laughing stock of her friends too!?*

"Anyway, what can I get you today?" She asks but doesn't wait for a reply, instead she jovially continues.

"I advise that you stick to something light coloured... we don't want a repeat performance of last week now, do we." Now she's laughing so hard that I want to punch her in the mouth. *Oh she's got an evil little streak in her, I don't like her one little bit!* I look at her name tag 'Rita'. *Hhhmmm not the name I would have given her.* She looks much more like an 'Arabella' to me. She's got quite a common accent, a naturally pretty face, mad black and pink hair and a body to die for... bitch! So 'Arabella' it is. 'Annoying Arabella' or 'AA' for short.

"I'll have a pot of a tea and some carrot cake please." I reply curtly, causing her to raise a sarcastic eyebrow and I instantly kick myself because I'd forgotten my plan of not eating anything!!

"Oohh... risky but it's your choice." She grins and disappears *thank god!*

But it's not long before she's back with my order and, as she leans across me to place the cake on the table she pretends to slip, as though she's about to drop the cake into my lap but then saves it. *Very funny... not!* Then she's off again, laughing loudly as she goes and I stare into her back wishing she would just piss off!

I decide not to dwell on this annoying women any longer and I look around the room for my first 'victim'. There aren't that many people here right now. Just a couple holding up their purchases to show each other their goodies. A Mother, enjoying what I imagine is a rare hot cup of coffee, whilst her daughter is asleep silently in her funkily coloured push chair. An old couple reading papers whilst sharing a pot of tea and in the corner, by the window, a man sitting quietly tapping away at his laptop.

I study him, he's wearing pin stripped trousers and a shirt that is unbuttoned slightly at the neck. He's fairly good looking but not striking, just kind of ordinary. He occasionally looks up to see who's around and then looks back down again and continues with his work. I give him a nickname 'Mr. Ordinary' or 'Mr. O' for short.

While I sit there, I gaze out of the window and see the two old ladies from last week's visit pass by. Maud, the bossy one way is out in front, empty handed. Whilst Madge, the quiet one, follows behind struggling with the pairs' granny trolley, which is bulging at the sides with what I imagine are Maud's bargains and not her own. I wonder whether the two 'M&M's *(my new name for them)*, come here every day, just to get out or whether it's purely a coincidence so see them here again today?

As I'm watching them, a lady enters the coffee shop and instantly she has my attention, because frankly she looks rather slutty.

Her blonde hair sits neatly in a high bun secured by a bright red Japanese wooden chopstick, her lips match in colour. She is wearing a black mini skirt that barely covers her behind, exposing her suspenders and only three of the buttons of her tight white shirt are fastened, meaning that you can't help but notice her gigantic boobs, that are only just covered.

'Ms. Slutty' sits down on the next table in front of 'Mr. O', placing her handbag at her feet whilst she positioning herself directly opposite him.   She summands the waitress and on hearing her voice 'Mr. O' immediately looks up and discretely rearranges his laptop, so that he can view her without it looking too obvious.   *Bloody pervert!*

She places her order and a few minutes later the waitress hands her a red fruit smoothie and a chocolate eclair.   She runs her hands over her thigh as she reaches down into her handbag, pulling out a mirror and a lipstick which she re-applies before placing them both back into the bag, all the while staring straight at 'Mr. O'.   When she begins to suck on her straw seductively I nearly spit my tea out in shock! Her Botox filled lips look like something out of a porn movie.   I glance over to him.   Every two minutes or so he looks up awkwardly, catches her eye and then quickly looks back at his keypad again and at first I feel a bit sorry for the poor guy as his face is becoming increasingly sweaty.   I notice the music playing quietly over the sound system and can't help but smile to myself when I realise that it's the soundtrack from the Diet Coke ad: 'I just wanna make love to you', by Etta James.

When she has finishes her drink, 'Ms. Slutty' pulls the wooden hair stick from her bun and moves her head from side to side, releasing her long wavy locks.   As though in slow motion, she then picks up the cream cake, takes a bite and allows the fresh cream to oozes out onto her lips and down chin.   She slides her tongue across to retrieve it, her eye's still remaining firmly fixed on 'Mr. O'.   *Gross, surely that's going to curdle in her tummy!?*

I return my stare back to him again and as I do so feel rather silly to have felt pity for him because he's actually openly enjoying himself now as he watches her. But it's all too much for him and two minutes later, he hurries off to the toilet, riskily leaving his computer on the table and not reappearing until quite a while after she has paid and left, looking rather flushed.

After this, I'm not sure whether to look over at him and scour or to avoid all eye contact but after a few moments of contemplation choose the later, I'm sure he's probably not bothered what I think anyway. *I knew he was a pervert!*

It's 'clubs' night tonight and so as not to cause suspicion I leave after a few hours of 'spying', to ensure that I am home and organised in good time. On the way out, I spot a lovely top and decide that I *have* to have it. Maybe I'll wear it to our anniversary meal on Friday?

Mental note - To go straight in and hide the bag at the back of the wardrobe, otherwise it'll be obvious where I've been and Dick will start asking questions again.

I pick everyone up and then drop them all off again to where they should be and decide to pop into Mercy's for a small glass of wine and a catch up when I collect John, as I didn't get see her on the weekend. The pair have a ritual of playing pirates, followed by dinner, followed by something arty and so when I arrive, John is painting dinosaurs while Mercy looks shattered.

She tells me how she had to work the entire weekend in preparation for a client presentation, only for it to be cancelled this morning and, for the millionth time I lecture her about changing her job. I also promise her that I will make it my mission to find her 'the perfect job' if she's not going to do it herself. And, as a start, to help her out *(obviously not for selfish reasons)* I con her into being my 'personal proof reader' as I write my book, I sell it to her as a 'temporary unpaid hobby-job' that she can do just for love.

"Oh yeah, how's the 'secret writing' going?" She enquires, honestly interested.

"*Well,* I haven't started actually started writing much down yet but I have been doing LOTS of research!" I admit. "Funnily enough I have been to a coffee shop today actually."

"Ooohh seen anything interesting happen, anything inspirational?" She asks, smiling devilishly.

"Well, funny you should say that...." I say and go on to tell her all about the George and Ophelia drama, about how 'Ms. Slutty' drove 'Mr. O' crazy and we cry with laughter, totally ruining Monday club for John! So I make a promise not to stay next week, so that he can have her all to himself. Mercy then rightly points out that I can't spend my entire time snooping on other people, I really should make a start on some actual storylines of my own and as usual, I take her advise on board.

I spend the rest of the week sneaking off to bed early, complaining of a headache or that I'm tired, just to secretively read 'creative writing' books. And by day, my writing finally commences, pushing my actual 'work' to one side... but I just can't help myself, the more I write, the more I'm enjoying it! I actually find that I'm rushing my day-to-day activities even more than usual, so that I can get back to my laptop and into my little make believe world.

I begin to look into different authors, literary agents and publishing companies. I pull the very few books that I have read down from the loft and off of the shelves, to discover that with the exception of just a few, most are written in a very similar in style, even the images / text on each of the book covers are alike. I find an article that mentions the importance of having a good 'synopsis'. *What the hell is a synopsis?* I have to look it up on the internet and to my surprise I find that I have already done it.. *woohoo god I'm good!* I read about 'query letters', something I had NEVER heard of before either and have to admit that initially I'm a bit unnerved by how out of my comfort zone I am.

During my investigations though, I think I've only gone and found Mercy the job of her dreams. She would make THE BEST literary agent! That night I phone her excitedly...
"Right, you know I promised that I would make it my mission to find you a new job? Well, I've only gone and bloody done it - how good am I!?" I state, over dramatising the facts slightly.
"You should count your lucky stars to have such a great sister as me, ya know!" I continue before she can speak.
"Really, what's that then?" She replies, *much* more unenthusiastically than I would have liked and I can tell by her tome that she thinks I'm about to wind her up and sasy something like 'a face double for Miss Piggy' or something equally as insulting and she's right to be suspicious because usually this may be the case, but not today.
"You are going to be.... der der der der da..... a Literary Agent!" I confidentially inform her, feeling extremely pleased with myself and before she can open her mouth, I'm off again.
"I just know that you'll be absolutely great at it. You read more than anyone I know *and* not all the same style of books either. You work hard. You are a good negotiator. Everyone comes to you for advise and... need I go on?!"
"Hhhmmm, actually that does sound quite interesting. I'll look into it in a bit more detail and let you know how I get on." She says much more enthusiastically now and I believe her, so leave any further lectures about her current job for another time.
"You better bloody do! I might need you one day no negotiate my terms." I joke.
"Alright bossy-flossy, I will!" She laughs back at me and I imagine her rolling her eyes at the other end of the phone.
"Anyway, what are you up to tomorrow? Do you fancy a lunch partner?" I ask her, already knowing that her response will be a yes because she rarely gets time for an actual break for lunch.

"Oh yes please! Shall we meet at the Cricks? At say 12.30?" She says and I can tell that she's pleased.

"Cool, I'll print you off some info and we can talk about it in more detail then and I'll give Patsy a tinkle too, to see if she's free".

"Okay, I'll see you then." She says before hanging up.

"Yeah, see ya."

I put the phone down and then immediately start dialling Patsy's number. I hear Dick groaning to John and Henry in the front room that I'm on the phone again and from the office, Lloyd is happily singing at the top of his voice as he fires up the laptop '2, 4, 6, 8.. even numbers are just great!'

I move to the kitchen, in an attempt to rid myself of all of their noise and have at least one phone call in peace, without interruption. *No chance!* I dial Patsy's home number and as I do, wonder why I'm bothering as no-one ever answers it.

"Who are you calling now? Not your bloody Mother again?!" Dick calls out, as he follows me around the house. *Oh go away!*

"No actually, I'm calling Patsy if you must know. I want to see if she fancies lunch with me and Mercy tomorrow."

"Oh right. You have such a hard life don't you, while I'm out at work grafting." He says playfully.

"Piss off! I work too you know." I snap. He's managed to wind me up, as no doubt was his intention.

"Ah, I can get you every time!" He laughs, pleased with himself and quickly disappears, before I lynch him again.

As predicted, no-one answers the home phone and so I try Patsy's mobile instead and she answers so quickly I wonder whether it even rang.

'Hiya."

"Hi. Do you fancy meeting up tomorrow for lunch?" I ask.

"Yeah, what time?" She asks and I can hear the front door to her Victorian house, slamming shut.

"12.30 in the Cricks."

"Okay, I'll see you there. Gotta go, I'm running late for yoga!" She says hurriedly, trying to get me off of the phone.

"Didn't you go to yoga this morning?" I ask, slightly confused and wondering whether I had messed my days up. "Yes I did but there's a new class tonight and I want to try it out." She says quickly and I know that it's my queue to go. "Oh right, no worries, I'll see you tomorrow then." I reply as I hang up. *I couldn't think of a worse way to spend my evening! My bending and stretching involves cuddling and bending down to pick my glass up.*

"Good god, that was the quickest phone call you have ever made!" Exclaims Dick, as he comes back into the kitchen again with a look of shock on his face.

"Did you call the wrong number?!" He questions jokingly. *Haven't you got anything better to do?!*

As I place the phone down, he picks it up and checks for a dialling tone before looking back at me, still wearing a shocked expression of his face.

"You're such a twat." I laugh and pretend to give him a filthy look.

"See, I make you laugh everyday!" He calls out laughing, as he leaves the room again.

"Hhhmmm... I don't know about that." I mumble to myself under my breath, as I resentfully start making tomorrows packed lunches for everyone, which has to be THE worst job on the planet! I could make Lloyds in my sleep with my hands tied behind my back, there are just two very boring variations. So with Dick and John's lunches I try to be creative - I cook pasta, make avocado, mayonnaise with lemon, cracked pepper and turkey sandwiches, ploughman's, wraps, the list goes on.

But Dicks pack-ups always have an extra little twist... just to make him appreciate how much effort goes into this job, that I loathe, I like to take a little bite out of his sandwiches each day. This act ensures that he remains fully aware of how good I am to him and reminds him never to forget his lunch because if he does, he won't ever have another made for him.

What he doesn't realise is that sometimes, if the boys are keeping me company in the kitchen when I'm on packed lunch making duties, I let them take the bite too... *little things hey!*

7

No more lies, no more creeping around!

The next day, we all meet up at the bar inside the Cricketers, at 12.30pm as arranged.   We would usually meet outside of pubs but being that we are 'old girls' and who have been coming here since before we weren't actually old enough to drink and can remember back to the time when the pub had separate 'social' and 'public' bars, it feels comfortable to enter alone.   The space has since had a lot of work done to improve it, it has been knocked through to form one big room, extended, updated, a smoking area added and god knows what else, sadly resulting in it losing a bit of its old character in our opinion.

As you walk though the double doors into the space, the bar is located to the left hand side and is peppered with numerous blackboards, highlighting this month's promotions, dates of performances and an itinerary of when they will be showing sporting events on the big screens.

The central area is a raised platform and has half a dozen oversized chairs which, in my opinion are a bit of a waste of space. *Surely the more chairs the better, when there's a room full of drunk people?*

The majority of the seating though, lies hidden behind this platform at the rear of the space and is less grand and showy. Without any discussion necessary, the three of us head in this direction.

We sit down at a table and open our menus, which offer the generic selection typical of this chain, nothing offensive but equally nothing over exciting either. *I wonder whether the chef is ever allowed to actually cook anything or if his/her talents are stunted at warming up part-cooked food, preparing sandwiches and pouring coffee?* We make our choices and order our food at the bar, forgetting as always to make a note of our table number and so I pop back to confirm.

We chat as always, from the minute that we meet until the time that we leave, with no pauses in between and no subject is off limits. This ability to find things to talk about exasperates Dick, who frequently rants about the fact that our family can speak on the telephone for an hour or so and then meet up that or the following day and still find more things to talk about.

After about half an hour, I cross the raised area to nip to the loo and on the way back, I spot my Mother-in-law relaxing in one of the oversized chairs, with a group of her friends, I suspect that they are from one of the many clubs that she attends. She looks a little bit sozzled, so I know that she's been here a while. *I can imagine that in about an hour's time, she will be sitting on her sofa, head back, snoozing and intermittently waking up asking 'Did I snore?'*

Rose is in her early seventy's. She's always well turned out and a complete socialite, usually eating out at least once a day. She loves life and enjoys being centre of attention with her silly jokes and impressions, that have people in fits of laughter. The boys lovingly refer to her as their 'Nutty Nana'. She has a boyfriend who is lovely too, although their personalities couldn't be more different. Frank is quiet and doesn't like being cooped up. If allowed, he would spend hours pruning his allotment, his kind nature meaning that with every visit, comes a bag of his personally home-grown fruit and veg. *For some reason, Henry can't quite grasp the fact that Frank is his Granddad and that he's male as he always greats him by saying 'Aunty Frank!', much to the amusement of the other too.*

I sneak up on her from behind, making her jump and she spills a little of her wine over her boobs.

"Oh ya bugger!" She yelps as she stands to kiss and cuddle me, before taking her seat again.

"Now I look like I'm lactating!" She giggles and all of her friends laugh along with her too.

"Hiya." I smile, as I receive my greeting.

"What are we all celebrating today ladies or is it just a catch up?" I ask no-one in particular, as I look around to see who she is here with.

"It's the 'Doing's club' isn't it!" She replies, also looking around at the other women in the group and then back to me, confused that I don't know this fact. But even after being with her son for nearly eighteen years, I'm still unsure how the 'Doing's club' ever started, what's involved or how you become a member? My suspicion is, that it may just be a name for that particular group of women to use as an excuse to have lunch together every now and then and that the name is just a formality.

"Who are you here with love?" She enquires and looks around the pub.

"Mercy and Patsy, we're sitting just over there." I say, pointing a finger in the direction of my sisters, who are looking over to see who I'm speaking to. They wave when they see Rose.

"Oh that's nice love." She smiles, as she waves back at them.

"Good job I'm not with another fells isn't it?" I laugh.

"I wouldn't blame you if you were." She jokes before adding.

"Just don't go having any more kids will you?" She says sighing and pretending to look exhausted, while her friends are all giggling again.

"Don't worry, I don't have the energy for an affair. I have to remember to do it with Dick once a week to keep him happy, I'd much prefer five minutes to myself a week over sex any day!" I jest starting them all off again.

"Oh too much information, you're so rude... but I'm with you on that one!   I'll come over and say hi."   She says, standing up with a slight wobble so that she has to steady herself by holding onto the massive chair back.   But just as she does so, Frank enters through the main doors and so we all remain where we are.

"Hi Frank, are you here to collect these lovely young ladies?" I saying smiling at him and he immediately returns a smile.

"They are neither young nor ladies, I can assure you!" He replies bravely and is then prodded and poked childishly in the ribs by a few of them.

Rose has recently cut down on the amount of driving she does and so poor Frank is more often than not a taxi to her and all of her friends, all of whom are usually a little bit tipsy by the end of their lunches, so I can only imagine that the conversations on the journeys home are typically quite blue. We say our goodbyes and I promise to say 'hello / goodbye' to the girls when I get back to the table, which I do and we continue our lunch together and when we leave, we all note how nice it is to catch up without the presence of our annoyingly loud children and agree that we must do it more often.   On the way out I hand Mercy the information that I have collated for her and between the three of us, we have come up with a game plan for her new career path for which we require daily updates.

Mental note - To ask Mum and Dad along too next time, they would have loved it here today!

I decide to be just as strict with myself this week too and by Friday, the first few chapters of my novel have been created, ready for my personal 'proof readers' to look over and critic *(plural because I have now also sweet talked Patsy into this role too).*

I am feeling *extremely* pleased and looking forward to rewarding myself tonight, as it is mine and Dicks 11th wedding anniversary and so we are *(much to the disgust of the boys)* going out for a fancy meal whilst they have a sleepover at Patsy & Greg's house. Something that they are so over excited about!

They have repeatedly asked since I collected them from school, what time we can leave and it's doing my head in. So much so that I eventually give in and drop them off as early as is acceptable, without taking the piss.

After a quick cup of tea and a catch up with Patsy *(the tea is offered by Patsy but made by me, as she always gets distracted half way through)*, I return home and attempt to get myself dressed up for the occasion. I take a long shower in peace, just because I can! I then get dressed, do my make-up and straighten my hair; even though I know that I will wear it up because it gets on my nerves when I wear it down.

I imagine that the topic about my hair always being tied up has featured in many a conversation for one or two of the more image conscious Mums on the school run, who have already pointed out to me that I should wear some brighter coloured clothes, rather than my difference shades of black. But fashion has never really ever been of much interest to me to be honest. The majority of my friends when I was growing up were boys and so I never had to dress up to impress them and this laziness has stuck. The majority of my friends now are girls but they all know me well enough to realise that they should feel very privileged, if I wear high heels or god forbid a skirt out on an occasion.

Mental note - To try harder with regards to my daily appearance!

Tonight though, I have taken my new top that I brought the other day out of hiding and as I try it on for the first time, I like it, I'm very happy with my impulse buy! Now there's just the question of whether Dick will notice that it's new or whether I can spin a yarn and cross my fingers that I'll get away with it. I often wear clothes that aren't actually new and he asks whether I have been hiding them at the back of my wardrobe for ages... it just so happens that on this occasion he would be right in thinking that. It only takes ten minutes for Dick to be ready, meaning that after a ten minute taxi ride we arrive at the restaurant just slightly before our reservation.

The restaurant's location is beautiful, it sits on the top of a hill overlooking the countryside and so I have requested a table in the conservatory, so that we can watch the sun go down. *I can be romantic from time to time!* As we enter, we are shown to a small area where we can order some drinks whilst we wait for our table. The interior, which seats around forty five diners I would guess, has white washed walls, wooden flooring / furniture and is cleverly set out over two areas, with the conservatory at low level and the main dining area raised by a few steps, so that everyone can enjoy the sights without having to stare through the other diners tables. There is a choice of A La Carte and a vegetarian / vegan menu's both of which are pricey for the area but we were well aware of this in advance, as we have eaten here before and the experience is as much part of the meal as the food itself.

With drinks in hand we are shown to our seats and asked which menu we would like and without any discussion necessary we both request the A La Carte. There are only a handful of dishes for each course but the clever descriptions make them all sound wonderful and after just a few minutes, we have already made up our minds, neither of us realising until this point just how hungry we are.

I decide on the goats cheese and caramelised onion tarts, followed by a medium cooked sirloin steak with peppercorn sauce and a side order of skinny fries. Dick opts for the prawn satay, followed by the mixed grill with Béarnaise sauce and a side order of dauphinoise potatoes. Then to speed the first course along, we both agree to look at the desert menus later, when we can judge if we are too full to challenge a rich pudding.

We are having a lovely time! We have admired the stunning views by day, watched the sun go down, the moon come up and now the darkness of the night gives the restaurant a very romantic feel.

We recall the memories of our wedding and what a lovely day we had, whilst we clink our glasses and toast to another year of marriage together and wish for many more to come. All of a sudden I hear a familiar voice. I look around the restaurant, trying to figure out where it is coming from and who it could belong to, I ask Dick and he hasn't got a clue, he just tells me to ignore whoever it is anyway. Then, as I look towards the bar again, I catch a glimpse of her... it 'AA'. *Arh why can't I get away from this bloody women!!!* I shrink in my chair, willing her not to see me and pray that she has booked to sit in the main area.

To my relief she has, along with thirteen of her friends male and female, taking up nearly half of the restaurant and the noise levels instantly increase, putting a bit of a dampener of the romantic ambience. I just know that she will spot me and humiliate me again and so decide that now's time to let Dick in on my secret writing, before she blows my cover!

"You know I said that I was going to write a book." I start, fiddling with my glass like a small child.

"Yeah." He replies and rolls his eyes and I'm unsure whether this gesture is at how I have suddenly changed the conversation and expected him to keep up or because I have mentioned the book again but I continue with my confession anyway.

"Well... I am actually doing it." I state, still looking at my glass.

"Doing what?" He interrupts impatiently and his reaction slightly annoys me.

"Writing my novel." I say looking up at him, trying not to let the annoyance show in my face.

"Oh! Does it take long to write a Peter and Paul book?" He jokes.

"Very funny." I say, narrowing my eyes at his sarcasm and kicking him underneath the table making him yelp.

"Actually, I'm on chapter three already and I'm really enjoying it!" I state very proudly. *I will not let him make this into a big joke, I've worked hard at this.*

"Oh good but are you any good at it?" He ask, half interested now and trying to make his face look serious although I can tell that he wants to make fun of me.

"Well, Mercy and Patsy have been proof reading it and they think so." I say, a bit more relaxed and pleased to have run my work past them just the other day.

"They wouldn't really tell you if you were crap though would they?" He laughs, scrunching his nose up.

"Well actually, yes they would! I've asked them to be very honest" I kick him again and then pause feeling slightly put out before sitting upright, straightening my napkin across my lap and continuing.

"So that I don't look like a tit if I'm crap." I admit.

"Anyway, we're always honest with each other and they've given it to some of their friends too, who've have enjoyed it too". I state proudly.

"Well, if you think you're going to make us millions, then you crack on love." He grins and reaches over to hold my hand and I'm touched by his support at long last. He then turns his head, gazes out of the window and his smile fades, leaving him looking slightly upset, which worries me. *Good god, I hope there's nothing wrong, he's rarely this serious!*

"Actually it's a bit of a relief" He confesses, still looking out of the window. *Tell your face will you!*

"Oh really, why?" I ask intrigued.

"Well, I have to be honest... I thought you were having an affair." He explains and I'm instantly relieved that it's nothing more serious but at the same time upset that I've lied to him and made him feel like this.

"What on earth made you think that?" I question him although I'm fully aware that I have been acting a bit secretive lately.

"Well, what with all of those early nights and headaches, I knew you were hiding something!" He elaborates.

"Why didn't you say anything?" I question him, feeling guilty.

"I was going to..." He says and then pauses, still looking out of the window.

"But I didn't know how to." He admits.

"And then the other day, I was chasing the cat out of your wardrobe and found the top that you're wearing now, stashed away, still in its bag with the labels on." I giggle and instantly feel bad for doing so but he ignores it anyway and carries on.

"I know that we joke about you hiding your new clothes but I thought you were saving it for your 'other man'." With this I let out a loud laugh. A slightly too loud laugh I realise, as his face instantly returns to stare at mine and then around the rest of the room, as if to see if anyone else it staring at us following my outburst.

"It just goes to show that we should always be honest with each other doesn't it?!" I say lightly, whilst trying to give him my best 'I'm-sorry-for-lying-but-I-promise-I'm-not-having-an-affair' kind of smile.

"Yes it does, no more lies and no more creeping around!" He replies sternly as a smile returns to his face and he squeezes my hand before admitting.

"In truth, I was shitting myself!" He admits.

"I couldn't imagine life without having to deal with one of your daily dramas or without opening my packed lunch to find a bite taken out of my sandwiches every day." He laughs and as I join him in laughter, he says.

"See, everyday! I make you laugh everyday... you really are living the dream girl!"

We stare at him for a while and study his face. His hair is almost all grey now and his cheeks a little wobblier than when we first met but he is still very attractive. I wouldn't hurt him on purpose and feel bad to have unknowingly made him feel this way. *I will include him in my activities from now on.*

Mental note - To never keep secrets again, not even little insignificant ones... a lie creates a lie!

As with Mercy, I go on to tell him all about the 'M&M's, about how Ms S seduced Mr O, about what happened when I spied on George and Ophelia. I tell him how irritating Rita can be and my new name for her and he listens to my stories with interest but is also with utter shock that I have managed to keep it all a secret from him for so long. Across the restaurant I point Rita out amongst the other diners and he pretends to get up to introduce himself so I throw my napkin at him in mock anger. He agrees that she does look more like an 'Annabelle' than a Rita' and whilst we listen to the laughter coming from their table, he jokes that she's telling them all about the nosy, pervy women that 'looked as though she'd shit herself', while I kick him for the third time tonight under the table.

When it's time to leave we're quite drunk. After settling the bill we tiptoe past her table, collect our coats and wait for our cab outside of the restaurant, where we both pretend to be undercover spy's, leaning up against walls with our invisible guns and jumping out on each other, totally forgetting that the restaurant has floor to ceiling windows overlooking that area and so I think it's safe to say that we managed to both lower the tone and look like idiots in the process but who cares, we've had such a good night. *And seriously, by the time that we can afford to come back, they won't recognise us anyway!*

On opening our eyes Saturday morning, it feels as though a bus has driven over our bed whilst we were asleep. I'm the first one to move and so, after taking a few tablets out of the box of paracetamol for myself, I hand it over to Dick. We then force a bowl of cereal down our necks, shower and wait a while to ensure that the alcohol has worn off enough to drive, before collecting the kids. We don't stay long at Patsy and Greg's and just by looking at the state of us both, they fully understand our reasons why. Thankfully the kids obviously had a late night too, as they don't put too much of a fight up about coming home, which we are *so* grateful for! When we get back, we sack the idea of tackling this week's homework much to the thrill of the boys and instead opt to watch films all day, while me while Dick drift in and out of our sleepy hangovers. I feel so bad all day that for the first time ever I can't even be bothered with the lottery choices/explanations and so without telling anyone, re-play last week's numbers to ensure that we are still in the game.

Mental note - To try to be more of a responsible parent by not getting so drunk every time I go out without them!!!

Sunday morning I wake up and still don't feel one hundred percent and neither does Dick, we must be getting old, we can't handle the drink anymore! So we decide plough through the kids homework and then go swimming and to my surprise, it actually makes me feel better... *maybe exercise is good for me?!*
Mental Note - To lead a more healthy lifestyle!

8

My wonderful (although distracting) friends!

The beginning of the week goes well, I'm half way through chapter five of my novel. I've given it a name and have re-read everything that I have written so far, amending lots of errors in past and present tense and I must admit, I'm secretly chuffed with myself. So I allow Dick to read this draft, safe in the knowledge that he couldn't do any better himself.

But, Wednesday comes along and as I sit in front of my computer nothing is coming to me?! *God not now, I was doing so well!* After a lot of self doubting, I decide to give writing a miss for the day, considering it as an act of someone or something higher, trying to tell me to get on with some of my actual paying work *(which is now pilling up and needs to be sorted through)*.

Thursday, the same thing... nothing?! *Eeekkk!* So again, I battle to clear the backlog of work I have whilst reassuring myself that I've done really well. Maybe I just need a bit of inspiration, to help me along a bit? In the back of my mind I go over what the creative writing books say about how you should try to write for at least half an hour a day, even if it is utter rubbish that you later delete and I panic a little bit. *Come on, come on, I can't admit defeat now, it'll be ammunition for Dick for life!!!*

I decide to take action... I need help.

A chance for another little spy-time maybe?   With that, I pick up the phone and call two of my closest girl friends, arranging to meet up at the local garden centre for lunch as I need to pick up some flowers for Mum. *Whatever happened to meeting in pubs, I miss those days SO much!!*   Now it's coffee, not wine that accompanies my lunch *(boohoo)* you can't really pick your kids up at 3.30pm smelling of alcohol can you? *Can you?!*   I arrive, late of course and they're waiting outside for me in the rain. *CRAP!!*   As we approach them, I open my mouth to apologise but they get in first.

"You made the arrangements for today and you're still bloody late!!!" Roxy scolds me and I can tell by the dampness of her hair that she's been waiting a while.

"Sorry. You should have gone inside and waited, rather than getting wet out here." I say, wrongly thinking it would help the situation.

"What and have you out here waiting for us, while we wait inside for you?"   She argues as we head through the electronic doors and go inside.

"No, next time we've agreed, we're just going to leave at the time we're supposed to meet you.   That way we should all arrive at the same time."   She concludes, as we walk past the flowers and I'm reminded that I need to stop here on the way back.

"Yeah Eva... naughty girl!"   Alexis pipes up, smiling as she winks at me.

Alright!!   I honestly wonder whether they have been watching my house; as I did only notice the time approximately two minutes before we were due to meet and so had to run out, coat in hand, like a women possessed to get here for this time, albeit very late.

Mental note - To try harder to be on time when meeting people, it's so rude to always be late - I was always on time pre-children!   I saw on social media recently though that there is a name for my condition, it's: 'Tidsoptimist': a person who is always late because they believe they have more time than they do.

"I'll buy the coffee's to make up for it" I smile sweetly.

"No, don't worry I've got my voucher." Says Roxy.

This particular chain of garden centres offers the chance to become a member for £10 per year. This membership then entitles you to receive a discount off of your purchases, as well as a monthly voucher for two free cups of coffee.

"You've still got mine too, haven't you? Enquires Alexis, watching Roxy as she rummages through her bag.

Roxy hands it to her without looking up as she continues to look for her own. She is like Alexis' PA. Alexis will often come up with an idea but it will be down to Roxy to see it through and make the relevant arrangements, it's a comical relationship but one that works in perfect harmony. So it's no surprise to me that she is responsible for looking after Alexis' vouchers as well as her own.

"You should have yours too Eva? You haven't forgotten them again have you?" She says, looking at me now with complete bemusement as I sometime look at my children but then having to smile at my crapness.

Arh yes I have!! This month's voucher can be found along with all of the others, in the corner of the cupboard, in the kitchen. Instead of my purse for some bizarre reason. Undoubtedly, much like the others, this voucher will only see the light of day, if by chance I actually remember to look at it before it has expired.

"I may have to entrust you with mine too" I laugh and they both agree that this would be the best idea.

Mental note - To move all god damn vouchers into my purse! Why I bother paying a year's membership I don't know, I barely ever make it out for breakfast or lunch and when I do, I always forget the sodding things! Not only that, I wouldn't shop here anyway because everything is so bloody expensive!

We weave our way through the maze of promotions and past the bakery, that smells absolutely wonderful and I consider stopping here instead of carrying on. Eventually reaching the cafeteria area at the back of the store, where we queue up like cattle at the food counter, with no-one daring to push-in with anyone else, for fear of being battered by the (so far) patient customers, who are getting more and more agitated the longer they are being made to wait. As standard there is only ever one person on duty here and this poor sod is in control of all of the hot and cold food, which spans as far as the eye can see, to the ever increasing queue of people waiting. When it's finally our turn, we tell the lady serving what we would like, who then advises us that, should we have a certain amount of items we will get a better deal. Something that always results in me, at least, walking away with a fat bastard portion of not very appetising food, that I didn't really want and will later regret eating.

You can guarantee that one of the two, over worked coffee machines will be out of action because of their constant use and today is no exception. Ironically, there are two members of staff disassembling and reassembling it whilst having a good old catch up. *Maybe one of them should leave the bloody thing broken and help out at the counter to speed things up a little!* Everyone *bar me of course* has coffee vouches to spend and so I am forced to make the decision of whether I still want to opt for a coffee, although I am fully aware that by doing so, after I have waited patiently for the working machine and then made it myself, my food will be cold. So instead I decide against it and have a cold drink. However, there is only one person on the tills too, taking more coffee vouchers than actual hard cash, which take an eternity to process and so my food is cold now anyway. *Aaarrrhhhh, it's SO infuriating... hire some more staff, you may be paying a wage but surely your profits will go up!!!!*

I remember now, why I hate this place so much. Why did I suggest coming here?! In the seating area there are two 'zones'. One is carpeted and usually home to more elderly folk, whilst the other has wooden floors which remind me a little bit of a school canteen and seems to attract the people with young children. *Maybe they don't want their kids to be held responsible for buggering up the carpet?* Both are always pretty full, every time I visit no matter what time of day, which never ceases to amaze me. As we are all childless today, we sit down in the quieter, carpeted side, where the tables aren't quite big enough for us all to place our trays down at the same time and so we have to take it in turns to unload our food, stacking the empties on a spare seat close by. Meaning that now our food is now so cold, it's almost inedible *(obviously we are the youngest in this zone by far)*. As we take our seats, we all realise that none of us have remembered to pick up any cutlery. So I quickly rectify this, by returning to the till area to collect a load of knives and folks, along with some condiments, to save us having to move again for at least an hour. We've got a lot of catching up to do!

Mental note - To save myself a tenner a year by cancelling my subscription for this place, it'll also save me (and others) getting cross with every visit!

Roxy's in the process of moving house and so we spend a while looking through the estate agents photographs, oohhhing and aarrhhing, asking questions and discussing her removal plans before then Alexis starts telling us a story. "I was going to give you 'Mucka', as a moving in present." She tells Roxy. *Noooo, not Mucka the Yucca plant?!* She has had this particular plant in her front room for as many years as I can remember, it's as much a part of the furniture as her sofa is and it h-u-g-e, taking up almost a quarter of the space. "Really!?" Gasps Roxy, obviously surprised and honoured all at the same time.

"Well, I figured that you'd have more space for him than I have, in your new massive posh house." She laughs which obviously embarrassing Roxy a little as her cheeks turn pink.

"Oh wow! Thank you, I am honoured!" Roxy exclaims, with a massive smile on her face.

"Oh hold on, don't get too excited." She continues, no doubt wishing that she had got to this part of the story a bit sooner, as now she senses that she is about to cause a lot of disappointment.

"Because you're not getting him now." She states, quite matter-of-factly.

"Oh right" Says Roxy, as the broad smile disappears from her face and is replaced by a slightly confused expression.

"No, Rhianna won't let me give him up." She says, passing the blame over to her lovely daughter and raising an eyebrow behind her slim black rimmed glasses, that she chose with the sole intension of looking more intelligent.

"You know what she's like. She 's always been very happy about being an only child, never lonely, just glad that she gets all of the bloody attention and money." She starts and you just know a funny explanation is about to follow.

"Yeah." We reply hooked, both trying to imagine what on earth could be coming next?

"Well, when I told her that I was thinking of giving you Mucka, she hit the bloody roof! She pleaded with me not to get rid of him. And why... I hear you ask?" And we both nod our heads.

"Well apparently he's been like a sibling to her?! She said that they've grown up together and that she couldn't think of anything worse than parting with 'him', that it would be just awful... I mean please!?!" She laughs affectionately at her daughters expense and we all join in, Roxy no longer feeling upset, just glad not to be splitting the 'family' up.

"I wonder where she gets her dramatic personality from?" I say, looking Alexis up and down and we all laugh again.

Alexis has had a tough life but it hasn't harden her in any way shape or form, she is still absolutely lovely! She has strawberry blonde hair *(not ginger!)* and a naturally friendly face. She's loud, proud and everything that a true friend should be! I could tell her just about anything, even confess to murder and I know she wouldn't raise an eyebrow or judge me. Instead just like Mercy, she would offer her reassurance and advise before rebuilding my confidence, leaving me feeling empowered and as though I could take on the world!

Roxy's more reserved than Alexis, with a massive heart and is also a true friend forever! She has dark hair, is slim and is loyal 'til the end! She will go out of her way for anyone that needs her help or advise and is solely responsible for ensuring that our group of friends have stayed in contact since secondary school. She is always the one to arrange our nights out and Birthday collections, even though at times I imagine it can be a pain in the arse for her but she never complains. She used to be a bit of a rebel at school and a few years ago, whilst I was in hospital for a month trying to ensure that my little calf-boy stayed put inside of me for as long as possible before making his dramatic entrance to the world, she reverted back to her school years by seeing how long she could get away with staying in my little side room for on each of her visits. One night she didn't leave until 10pm and I had visions of her running out and getting caught by the nurses. We laughed so much, she definitely cheered my time in there up!

Mental note - To always remember how lucky I am, to have such wonderful friends... even if they do distract me from my spying!

After lunch I return home, sit at my computer and begin writing and it's flowing again... *aahhh blockage cleared, there is a god!*

I tap away at the keypad all day and part of the evening until my family are all shouting at me from the front room, that they are hungry and need their curry fix and so I retire for the weekend, pour myself and Dick a glass of wine and order the curry.

On Saturday after the completion of everyone's homework, we gather together to chose this week's lottery numbers.

I choose: '1' The amount of good writing days I have had since sharing with Dick my news and question whether he is a bad omen. '4' The amount of days that the 'writers block' lasted for and '25' the amount of thousands of pounds I hope to win from last week's text competition that we entered.

Dick pleasantly surprises me, by choosing some different numbers this week and by having an explanation for each. He chooses: '1' The amount of fabulous nights out he has had with his beautiful wife. *Maybe it's him having the affair or he wants something, I'm not sure which?* '3' The amount of lovely kids he has *Okay, he's freaking me out now... someone bring back my husband!* And '27' the age where my beauty peeked. *Oh, there it is... back to normality, an 'insult-compliment', unintended but very typical of him none-the-less.*

Lloyd opts for: '41' As in forty one thousand pounds, which is how much he has heard that an online gamer can earn every year and so this is his new job preference. *Didn't we go through a similar theme a few weeks ago?* '24' The age he will start this new career and '6' the number of weeks left in this term before it is the holidays. He then carries on and on about what equipment he will require to do his job professionally i.e. a microphone, webcam etc. etc. and after five minutes of trying to act interested, I ignore him and move on to John, who like Dick has actually put more effort into this week's choices too.

He chooses: '2' The amount of times he has managed to sneakily slip into my bed and get away with staying there all night, because I have been too tired to move him and '5' because he has been good all week and not had his name moved from the sunshine picture. *This is a real achievement for him and he is so rightfully proud of himself!*

To explain, all of the kids from nursery right the way through to year two, start the day with their named photographs on the 'sunshine' picture but if they are naughty, it gets moved onto the 'rain cloud' and if they continue to be naughty, it's moved again to the 'thunder cloud'. However, should they redeem themselves during the course of the day, it can be moved back up and so on.

So, with everyone happy and in agreement, this week's lottery numbers are as follows + one lucky dip:

Line One: 1, 2, 4, 5, 25 and 41.

Line Two: 2, 3, 6, 7, 24 and 27.

Later that evening, as we take our seats in preparation for the draw, the cat 'Spud' jumps up next to me, as she always does when the noise levels die down.

"Spud. Spuddy! Spud-spud" Dick calls to her and then moans that how no-one ever sits with him. *Her name derives from the boys favourite dinner choice.*

"You know what you have to do" I say and look over to see him shaking his head.

"Just smile at her and she'll come to you!" I continue, smiling at her myself now as she tramples all over me, affectionately head butting my face before turning around so that I get an eyeful of her bum hole. *Gross!*

"As I tell you every time, I am not smiling at a bloody cat!" He says and returns his attention to the television but just moments later as she moves over to his lap, I catch him smiling at her and have to snigger but he pretends not to hear a he carries on stroking her, enjoying a bit of attention.

The balls are jumbled up and we eagerly await the results... but alas, no win for us again this week!

9

Stay away from the water's edge!

All caught up on my 'actual' work, I have decided to dedicate every day this week to 'people watching', in different locations around the local towns.   Today I am going food shopping first (so that I feel that I have contributed to my 'normal life' chores) and then I'm off to a little Spanish restaurant I know, about half an hour away that does wonderful tapas.   The idea behind choosing this location was because I know that I can just keep ordering single dishes and so stay for as long as I need to, without causing suspicion *or* looking as though I'm waiting to pick up a stranger.

Before I leave the house the phone rings, there's a problem with one of my jobs and so I spend the next hour and a half sorting it, meaning that by the time I have dressed (in a smart, knee high grey skirt, crisp white shirt and black high heels), the shopping goes completely out of the window because I'm now hungry and I drive directly to the restaurant.   I decided to take my laptop, so as to give the impression of being a high powered business women, much too busy to be drawn into idle chit-chat.

I park up in the multi storey car-park, within the newly regenerated part of the high street and walk the short distance to the restaurant.

As I pass the window, I glance in and notice that it's *very* dark inside and my stomach aches at the thought of having to find somewhere else to eat, but as I get closer I realise that it is open.   Now though I start to question whether if I should enter alone.   *Come on, I can do this!*
I stand in front of the double doors and take a deep breath before pushing them open.   On entering, I am greeted by an unmanned wooden podium at which I stand and wait, as instructed by the sign to do so.   Ten whole minutes past and I am still standing there like an idiot, whilst the other diners enjoy their lunches, so I decide to seat myself.   I have had time to study the space well by now and know exactly where I am going to sit - at the rear of the space, hidden away in a corner, like a real spy would.

Mental note - To be more proactive in future, don't wait around like a numpty for everyone to talk about and to research on my venues on the internet first to avoid eating in horrible places.

The walls inside are all orange, some painted, some tiled with pictures and posters plastered all over them. The furniture is wooden and there are dimly lit lighting pendants and wall lights in a vintage style, with black chains and off white opal diffusers.   It's nowhere near as nice here as I recall but it will do - I suppose it has probably been about six years since my last visit and by the look of it, it hasn't been updated since.
I sit down and wait for the second time what seems to be an age, before a young attractive man with a lovely Mediterranean tan *and* accent, finally emerges from out from the kitchen area.   He's wearing tight black trousers, which shows off his little pert bum and a short sleeved white shirt, unbuttons enough to allow his chest hair to creep over slightly.   He hands me a menu and apologises for the delay and then, as fast as he came, he disappears again.
After a few minutes he's back in front of me again though and I ask in my poshest, most 'business women' sounding voice:

"Would it be okay if, instead of having all of my tapas dishes served to me at the same time, they could be brought out individually? Only I have some work to do whilst I'm here."
"No problemo Senora!" He replies politely and smiles.
"Just tell me your order now.   Then give me a little wink every time you are ready for another dish and I bring to you." *Oh wow, he's quite sexy actually!*
"Oh, okay." I say slightly flustered at my own naughty thoughts and struggling to figure out the dilemma of whether I should actually wink at him each time or if I should just raise my hand or call him instead? *I'll figure that out later!*
"Today, we have an offer." He says, helpfully opening up the menu to full size and it is vast!
"You can have one item from the starter and four dishes from the tapas menu, for one fixed low price."   He continues, pointing to the different areas on the menu, while I inhale his mix of aftershave and sweat. *Hhmm.. I quite like it!*
"Okay, I'll go with that please."   I say as I study the menu, feeling slightly rushed and embarrassed that he is still standing over me, waiting rather than giving me some time alone to choose.
"Right. Erm. Yes okay, I'll have the rustic garlic bread, anchovies, the mixed meats, olives and paella please.   Oh and a white coffee with sugar."   I say before closing the menu and as I look up at him, I suddenly realise that I may have been a bit bullied into this choice, as it's far too much food for just one person to eat. *Maybe he just thinks that I'm fat?!*
"No problemo, for such a beautiful lady" He smiles and again he's gone, before I can amend my order.

Smiling to myself and feeling flattered by his last comment, I set my laptop down on the table using it as a cover tool, while I look around to find my first victims. The restaurant is filling up but I've hidden myself away so well that I'm having trouble seeing anyone or anything other than the kitchen and the toilet. *Oh bugger, I had the whole bloody restaurant to choose from too!*

I spot the waiter, 'Mr Handsome' returning with my coffee and garlic bread and so start typing and even though I know he is coming, as he places it on the table I jump with surprise. "Hhhmmm... you are looking at something you shouldn't be?" He asks with a wink. "I can see you are going to be trouble Missy!"

I definitely don't feel like a confident business women now, instead I feel more like a teenager being woo'd by a waiter whilst on holiday! Within minutes he's back, with my breads and olives together which really does shock me this time, from his past mañana attitude I hadn't expected to see for at least half an hour. *He obviously wasn't listening when I said 'separately' now was he?!*

Just then a group of around twenty men enter the restaurant, obviously on a works lunch to celebrate a Birthday, judging be oversized '30' badge that one of them is being made to wear, obviously under duress. 'Mr Handsome' helpfully re-arranges the furniture, by pushing tables and chairs together to form one long line, for them to sit together. The noise level has risen somewhat since the men have arrived and is increasing the more alcohol they drink. After a while, some of the couples start to leave, their romantic lunch dates obviously ruined.

'Mr Handsome' is enjoying the crowd and has regretfully become less attentive. I try to catch his eye to a few times but he hasn't even glanced my way for at least forty minutes and I must admit that I'm slightly disappointed and becoming increasingly annoyed.

I try a new technique of attracting his attention, by awkwardly waving at him and winking but have no joy and so instead get up from my seat and attempt to approach him. As I move towards the group, one of the men shouts out.

"Ah, you must be the stripper! Sorry, I saw you winking but it didn't dawn on me that you could have turned up early , I thought you'd come through the front door!!" He yells, getting out of his seat too. *The stripper?! Do I look like a bloody stripper?! After all of the effort I have gone to, I'm being greeted as a bloody stripper?!*

"No I am not the striper, thank you very much!" I state firmly trying to sound like a head mistress, whilst giving him a look to kill before continuing "And I wasn't winking at you, I was trying to get the waiters attention actually."

"Oh sorry love." He says half heartedly, as he looks around at his friends who are all killing themselves laughing.

"Apology accepted." I say, still frowning and am about to open my mouth to tell 'Mr Handsome' that I'm ready for my paella, when the guy pipes up once more.

"Wey-hey Manuel, I reckon you're in there!" He shouts out as I watch on, mortified!

"Don't fancy make a few quid then? Coz you've got a great pair of tits love!" He enquires, turning back to me again, in an even louder voice than before, sending his friends into roars of laughter.

Right that's it! "Oh fuck off knob head!" I snap, as I turn on my heel and march back to my seat to hide my now bright red and pulsating face behind my laptop screen, whilst praying for the world to swallow me up!

Across the room, I can hear' Mr Handsome' asking the group politely to keep their noise down. He then brings the (fated) paella over and makes an attempt to apologise on behalf of the men, but it's not working, I am still livid.

I tell him not bother with my food as I am leaving and request that he brings me the bill instead, which he does straight away, along with some vouchers for my next visit as a further apology and instantly I feel bad for him. I accept both and have to smile at his cute face, although I leave without tipping. On my way past the long table, I glare at the ringleader of the group, who responds by laughing at my expense again. *Twat!*

I am still furious when Dick comes in from work, I tell him the story of how my day has gone and he too cries with laughter, telling me that I can be his hooker anytime. I eventually see the funny side and he spends the rest of the evening winking at me and asking what my speciality is.

"It could only happen to you." He says sleepily as we lie in bed. He's obviously trying to picture the scene in his head, which is amusing him.

"I wouldn't mind, my character was supposed a business women, not a hooker. Think I'll have to rethink my outfit next time." I say, wondering where I went wrong with my disguise.

"Character?" He questions me, as he sits bolt upright.

"Yeah, I thought I might meet some different people than I would usually if I go to places in cognito." I tell him, playing it down.

"Oh kinky!" He says and raises an eyebrow. "You don't dress up for me."

I cover his head with a pillow and pretend to suffocate him.

"Next time, why don't you try dressing up as a dog. You'd be able to pull that one off." He says, his voice muffled by the pillow.

"Right that's it!" I laugh as I attack him once more.

"See I make you laugh everyday!" He reminds as he uses just one arm to fend me off.

"Hhmmm, I dunno about that?!" I mumble, as I submit and close my eyes to sleep.

The next morning, being that I didn't get around to doing it yesterday my one and only job is to go food shopping.   I wrongly decide to check out the newly opened supermarket, which results in it taking me the best part of the day!   When I'm not trying to avoid scary looking women, shouting at their friends or children in different isles to themselves, I'm hunting for items on my list because nothing was where you would expect it to be located.

Mental note - To never return to this hell hole!   I am no snob but this experience was enough to put me off for good, I feared for my own life at points!

On Wednesday I meet up with Mercy at the Cricketers again, Patsy can't make it today as she has a fitness class.   Mercy tells me that she had started researching the new career path that I was about to force her into but unfortunately decided that it's not for her and in fact she prefers the idea of becoming a teacher instead.   *Okay, I'm not so good after all!* We spend the time hatching a plan of how to tackle her dream, what her ideal position would be, who could help her reach this and work out how much money she needs to survive each month.

As standard we know a few of the people in here today, some of whom we say 'hello' to and some of whom we try to avoid making eye contact with, so as not to appear rude for not talking to them.   Today all of the usual suspects are in, the ones that drunk here when we were underage but whom still haunt the same space now in their forties and fifties.   In their youth most of these were part of the 'good looking group', the ones that everyone wanted to go out with but looking at them now, they look quite sad.   As though they have never moved on, that they are in a 'youth bubble' that should have popped years ago.

Some are married, some have kids but their 'drinking with their mates' routine has and will never be changed because that's what they've always done. *You've got to feel sorry for their families!* On our way out we exchange the usual pleasantries with them but that's as far as the conversation goes as we have little in common with them now.

Mental note - To remember how lucky I am that Dick is a 'homely' man. Even if, at times that particular trait can wind me up when I'm trying to motivate him!

On Thursday I decide to revisit the big shopping centre for another spy session. As I pass, I peer through the window of the coffee shop and notice that 'AA' is on shift *again* and so decide to avoid it for today. Instead I walk around for a while, making a few purchases mainly clothes for the boys but also toys, to re-stock the present bag. After a while my feet can carry me no further, so I stop for lunch in the food court. I pick up some hot Japanese Katsu Chicken with rice and head towards the rear of the space, where the ceiling height changes drastically opening up into a high atrium and making the space feel airy and spacious with big windows that overlook the pond and play area. Here feels in total contrast to the rest of the mall, which is closed in with few visible exits, designed to keep you from leaving.
I slump my tired body into a chair and as I tuck into my food, struggling with the complicated combination of chop sticks and rice I spot 'Mr O' *(the purve)* and he's with a women.
She is of similar age to him and they are with a child of around nine or ten. I assume that this is his wife and daughter, both are dressed quite conservatively in smart but pretty dresses. He appears totally uninterested with their conversation, as he studies his paper.

I watch while each take it in turns to try to win his attention, on numerous occasion, showing him their purchases and pointing out till receipts but to no avail and after about fifteen minutes, he checks his watch, kisses both on their foreheads and makes his way back to work or wherever he is headed.   Shortly after, the pair disappear too.   *I bet they'd be disgusted is they knew what had got him all hot under the collar a few weeks back!*

I remain seated for a further twenty minutes, studying eating habits of some off the other people but feel so worn out and stuffed, that in all honesty it's making me feel a bit sick, so I return to my car and make my way home.   I could quite easily curl up on the sofa and fall asleep now but I can't, I have to collect the boys from school.   I take the slip road and instantly hit a traffic jam.   *Bugger!*

"Please clear!   Please clear" I chant out loud to myself, over and over again like a mad women.

I look around at all of the other cars stuck like me, unable to get where they need to be.   I notice the beaten up bright red car next to me and as I examine it, I come face to face with the driver.   *Oh for god's sake, it's AA!*

I try to look away quickly but she's smiling straight at me. She has a pretty smile and so I find myself naturally smiling back at her, even though I really don't want to.   I try to turn away but out of the corner of my eye I can see that she's wound down her window and is gesturing me to do the same and as there is no movement in the traffic, I can't now pretend not to see her and so have no choice but to do as I'm told.   *This bloody women!*

"Hiya.   You just love this place hey?!"   She says brightly, still smiling and presumably referring to the shopping centre and not the traffic jam.

"Hi... erm, Rita isn't it?" I reply, having to stop myself for calling her AA and suddenly feel embarrassed to let her see that I have recalled this much information about her.

"Rita?"   She questions, before laughing.

"Oh, no I think you've got me muddled up with the other girl at the coffee shop." She tells me.

"Oh sorry." I start to apologise.

"It was just, the other week when... well you know when... when I had my erm 'spillage'... your name tag said..."

"Oh that ha, ha!" She interrupts chuckling to herself in realization.

"We sometimes swap name tags to confuse the olden's." She admits giggling. "Mean I know but it passes the time. My names actually Annabelle."

Mental note - To not take everything at face value... but that aside, how good am I - Annabelle, I must be bloody physic!

"Oh right! Hi Annabelle, I'm Eva." I respond politely, trying to curb my 'pleased with myself' grin, to avoid looking creepy.

"We seem to be bumping into each other a lot, don't we?" She says.

And I want to say 'yeah we do, unfortunately, you complete pain in the arse!' but instead say "Yes I suppose we do, small world hey."

"It is by chance isn't it?" She asks doubtfully and I can tell by her tome that she is actually studying my reaction in case I am. "I mean, you're not a weirdo stalker are you?"

"No you're safe, don't worry." I say and to my surprise can't help laughing at the irony myself now.

"Phew!" She says and pretends to wipe the sweat from her brow.

"I must admit, I was starting to think the same about you." I confess. *Little does she know that I've actually been trying to avoid her for the past few weeks.*

"Is that the reason that you asked me to open my window?" I quiz her, raising an eyebrow.

"Yeah." She says, as bold as brass and quite matter-of-factly before continuing. "I figured that it was better to confront you, rather than be left to wonder if I'm going to wake up with an axe in my head."

"Well, it's nice to meet you. We must live close to each other or something?" I conclude laughing and then instantly realising that this does actually sound like a stalkerish comment.

"I live in Rainham. That's Rainham in Kent, not Essex." I tell her, trying to redeem myself.

"Oh wow, me too! Moved there a few months ago!" She says excitedly and with that the traffic starts moving and so we say our goodbyes. *Hhmm small world!*

That night I am eager to update Dick on the 'AA' front and let him know what a physic genius I am, getting her name right. He on the other hand, is more impressed to find out that the person I have been actively trying to avoid thinks that I'm her stalker and mocks me for yet again being crap at being inconspicuous.

Friday is an inset day and so no school. So, to wear the kids out and with my Mum and Dad in tow, we have come to a beautiful park a short drive away, that is surrounded by four hundred and fifty acres of land, for a picnic and a kick about. After lunch, we watch whilst the boys play in the park and then the scooter park, before buying an ice cream and walking over to the thirty acre lake to feed the *(frankly spoilt and ungrateful)* ducks, with the loaf of bread that we have actually remembered to bring with us. I warn them that these particular ducks are so well fed they may not come over and all to stay away from the water's edge.

There are a few other kids hanging around empty handed and so I make my boys share some of their bread with them, so that no-one is left out. Lloyd immediately takes control and eagerly hands a piece to each of child. But this just serves to annoy John, who is visibly changing moods right in front of my eyes. I scold him and tell him to behave otherwise he'll have to go and sit in the car by himself.

I believe this to have done the trick and so sit back down and continue talking to Mum and Dad but seconds later, I hear a massive splash.   And to my utter disbelief, I look around only to discover that John has pushed Lloyd into the pond.   *The little shit!*

I jump up and pull an absolutely drenched Lloyd out of the water, all the while shouting at John, whilst glaring into his eyes as though I'm going to kill him... and he is very aware that he is in BIG trouble!   Everyone around the pond is now fixated with our little group, no doubt discussing what a bugger John has been.   The parents of the other kids that they have been talking to, now pull them aside in fear and I'm just thankful that it one of my own children that he has pushed and not someone else's!   I take Lloyds saturated t-shirt off and replace it with my own sweater.   I have nothing to dry him with and no clean bottoms for him to change into and am so livid that we have to call it a day and go home.

All of the way home I reprimand John; who has gone full circle - from initially being angry, to then being surprised and annoyed with himself, to reverting back to angry again.

And, as I look in my rear view mirror, I can see that he has his fingers in ears and is chanting "I'm not listening, I'm not listening!" to drown the sound of my voice out.   And my blood is boiling!   Both Mum and Dad stay pretty quite all of the way home too, making pleasant chit chat about the trees and the weather, as they sense that I'm about to lose the plot too and don't want to be responsible for tipping me over the edge.

As I drop them off they don't wait for kisses but instead practically run inside while I pull away head for home, at speed, where luckily Dick is home from work already.   And, after ordering John into the house and being totally ignored, I leave him in the car and tell Dick to deal with him before I do and it's obvious that he can instantly sense the tension and heads straight outside.

When he comes back inside, he tries to find out what has happened but the other two boys remain tight lipped and as quite as mice because they know that he'll start shouting too if they tell. I instruct Lloyd to go upstairs and run himself a bath, while I go into the kitchen and pour myself the biggest glass of wine.... *oh I need this! Bloody inset days!*
Needless to say, John missed out on curry night and instead earned himself an early night, with no bedtime cuddle from me. It was only later that evening my Mum called to check how everyone was *(and possibly to make sure that John was still alive and that I hadn't killed him)*, that I could finally see the funny side.

Mental note - To just keep telling myself that he has come so far and that this phase will be over soon... COME ON PMA, WORK!!!!

Saturday morning we all choose our lottery numbers in the same way as usual. I choose: '1' Being the number of times I have been mistaken as a hooker this week. '4' The amount of times that I have lunched out, to which Dick pipes up about what a hard life I have while he's at work. And, 10 the amount of times I have had to tell John off this month *(followed by a lecture about how he had acting being up until a while ago and how he should try harder again)*.
Dick's choices are: '13' Because it's 'unlucky for some' *(great omen then)?* '20' The average in pounds that each of my lunches have cost this week and '59' because he has used this number so often that he can't not use it anymore. I then explain the reason why we choose our numbers in this manner again to him but he's having none of it and remains fixed with his choices, rightly pointing out that I let Henry choose '7' each week. *I think Dick needs to grow up a bit!*
Lloyd is too interested with playing on the iPad and so yells out from his thrown (on the toilet).

"Just put me down for 38, 40 and 42... nice even numbers."
I don't push this any further, I'm just chuffed that it has
taken such little effort to prize the numbers out of him this
week.   John is still sulking and refuses to take part this week
and so I tell him that I have selected for him '2', the age he is
acting and '7' the number of days of the week he will have to
go to school if he were attending boarding school.
I then add '3' for Henry... his real age for once.   *See, up yours
Dick!*
So, with everyone happy and in agreement, this week's
lottery numbers are as follows + one lucky dip:
Line One: 1, 3, 7, 13, 20 and 59.
Line Two: 1, 2, 4, 10, 30 and 59.
But alas, after the big build up and the usual outcome, we
don't win a single bloody thing and are all slightly
disillusioned once again but at least John has finally come
out of his mood and has apologised to the entire family, so
life can resume as usual. He sits beside me all night, telling
me how I'm the best Mummy he's ever had and that he loves
me more than I could ever love him, which of course I
lovingly argue and then he does the same and so on until
Dick tells us both to be quiet or else he is going to put the
snooker on.

10

What is it with trains this week?!

I have a site meeting first thing on Monday morning and so arrive at the school gates nice and early, as I am hoping to catch the train that will get me to London with enough time to spare to grab some breakfast.   But as with all of my plans, this is already looking as though it's not going to happen. We enter Henrys classroom and I kiss him goodbye but, just as I turn to make a speedy exit I catch site of Henry and a few of his friends having a physical fight over a large train crossing sign and so have to hang back to pre-warn the teachers of its dangers.   They are all busy speaking to the other parents and so I have to wait patiently in line whilst cursing in my head that I'm going to miss my train.

Mental note - To talk to Henry about having 'kind hands' etc. to try to avoid him from having the same issues that John has had when he goes up into big school at the end of the year.
Subsequently after dropping the other two boys off, I miss my train... by a millisecond. *Arh!* I stand for a while, boiling hot and red faced after my sprint from the car park and watch it disappear into the distance.   *Great no nice breakfast for me then!*

I walk over to the station shop where the selection of food is rubbish, they offer no hot food and so I buy myself a coffee and some crisps, knowing that this will have to fill me up now until after my meeting. I then have to wait a full half an hour for the next train to arrive and when the doors open, I hop on to begin my travels. As I do so, I am instantly aware that I look very unglamorous compared to the other passengers, in my safety boots, high vis jacket, with hard hat in hand.

Result, I think to myself as I hurry to claim the one and only free seat in the carriage, beside an overweight business man next to the window. He's dressed very colour co-ordinately, in his grey suit trousers, stripy red and grey shirt and red braces. His matching jacket is draped over the adjoining arm rest which he makes no attempt to move, either when I sit down nor throughout the entire journey. *A bit rude!* Approximately half an hour into the train ride, there is a terrible smell that takes my breath away and I have to use all of my self control not to vomit. Eventually the smell fades and I can breathe again but within just a few minutes it's back again and I can suffer it no longer! With the toxic stench threatening to eat my insides, I stand up and make a dash for the train doors just as they open. *There is a god!* It's then that the penny drops that everyone around me must be regular commuters, to have left this particular seat empty. They too must have, at some point been put through the same initiation ceremony as I have just been through. When I get to the doors I gasp, madly inhaling and gulping at the fresh air as though I have just had my lungs aspirated. And, a few seconds later, feeling slightly embarrassed, I manage to compose myself and timidly look around the carriage, aware that I have maybe been just a bit too over dramatic. Blatantly I have, as there are people sniggering at me from all angles.

I cautiously look back over to where I had previously been sitting, aware that if the offender has witnessed my actions, they could be rather embarrassed too. *But seriously, they should learn to hold it in... that was just gross!* As I do so, I see the man in with the red braces straining his neck to stare around at me, with not the slightest look of embarrassment or anger as I had expected, instead he's actually smiling, a broad 'I'm pleased with myself' smile, whilst those around him are looking rather green. *This is obviously some kind of thrill to him. The dirty bastard!!!!*

Mental note - Only sit where others have moved from, if there are spare seats ask yourself why in future!

Another half an hour passes during which time I make no attempt to relocated my bum but remain standing all the way, and then finally we arrive at London Bridge. The doors of the carriage don't open straight away and out of the corner of my eye I can see Mr. Smelly fast approaching, his stubby little legs slapping against each other as he speed walks towards me, with his beaten up old briefcase in his hand. I stare out of the window, willing the lights to start flashing to indicated that the doors have been released but they don't. He reaches me and boldly stands right up next to me, so close in fact that I can feel his belly rubbing against my arm, something that makes my body physically shudder from, with no pre-warning and again I feel embarrassed. I take a side step and pretend to read an invisible text message on my phone.

"What's up with ya women? Don't ya think I'm sexy? He asks grinning, which reveals his disgusting yellow teeth which I stare at, whilst trying to figure out if I misheard what he had said.

"Do ya fancy grabbing some breakfast together" He continues in his thick Irish accent, as spit flies out of his mouth and I actively dodge it.

"Excuse me?" Are the only words that I can conger up, I can barely believe my ears.

"I said, do ya want a bite to eat with me" He repeats again, although slower this time as though he is talking to a deaf person.

"No I don't thank you." I say politely still in shock, which I imagine my face portrays too.

"Why?" He asks, as though he can't believe his ears.

"I'm married." I state, thinking that this will put an end to it.

"So?" He questions me again and I am quite frankly astonished!

"I don't ask twice women!" He says and winks at me. *You just have.. you repulsive pig!*

"I am *happily* married thank you!" I inform him again before offering some advise.

"And, quite frankly I think you should watch what you eat, something's obviously wrong in your diet to be producing that kind of smell, it really isn't something to be proud of!" I sniff at him.

"Oh it's me odour that has you looking at me like that, is it? It's only natural!" He says totally unashamed and instead he has a huge grin plastered all over his oversized face.

"What, you don't fart?" He questions me. *Oh Jesus, come on doors!!!!!*

"In private I do, yes. In private. However, at the ripe age of thirty eight I must say, I no longer find it very funny though?" I tell him but I haven't finished yet.

"And I have to say that I don't recall *ever* smelling that *bad!* I think you mister, need to go to the toilet!" I state in a motherly voice, looking at him with disgust. Fully aware that I am sounding like my Dad when me and sisters we small. Around me, I can hear the hushed giggles from some of the other passengers and so try to leave the conversation there, so as not to cause a scene. But he hasn't finished with me yet.

"It was just an ickle love puff" He laughs, an ugly loud laugh that makes me look away and grimace.

"I could smell ya pheromones ya see and thought I'd give ya get a wiff a my scent." He continues and I nearly puke in my mouth. *Oh my god, I have never spoken to such a vile person before in my life!*

"I can assure you that you could smell nothing of the sort!" I snap, totally grossed out.

"Whilst I, had to endure your death scent!" I say and as I do so, instantly realise that it came out way too loud as the girl next to me lets out an involuntary shrill and immediately covers her face to hide the tears of laughter that are now forming in her eyes. I want to laugh with her but I am so disgusted by this fowl man that I can't even look in her direction for too long.

"Oh come on now, it wasn't that bad." He says looking around for back-up from one of the other passengers, still humoured by his own gross actions.

"Not if your an animal, no." I say, whilst pushing the buttons in a feeble attempt to get the doors open and get myself out of there.

"Look at the poor people around where you were sitting. Look at the colour of their faces. And look at her!" I say, pointing my finger in the direction of a lady who has fallen asleep.

"You've knocked her clean out, someone should check that she still has a pulse!" I continue and instantly feel my cheeks redden even more, at my rudeness and now the entire carriage is listening in to our conversation with amusement.

"I like my girls to be tomboys." He continues, as though he hasn't heard what I have just said. *So now you're calling me a tomboy... for the love of god! I am about to go on site thank you very much, I don't always dress this way. Last week a hooker, this week a tomboy, why do I seem to attract all the bloody weirdo's!*

"They would have to be nose-less tomboys , to put up with that arse!" I retaliate, narrowing my eyes.

"And you don't get that many of them around do you? So you'll be single for a while!" I say childishly and with this, Little Miss Happy behind us is nearly on the floor, tears are streaming down her cheeks while she whimpers, trying to remain silent in her laughter but the more she tries, the louder she becomes and it's contagious, more and more people are beginning to laugh now not just at us but also at her and again I pray in my head for the doors to part.

"Okay, I'll take it as a 'no' then. Your loss." He says, quite brazenly. *Hallelujah he's finally got the hint!!*

"You can take it as a 'never'!" I add, just to make sure that he really does get the message.

"Stuck up your own arse, that's what you are. Frigid bitch, you can't take a laugh you!" He says rudely. *Me. Stuck up my own arse!?!*

"Well at least nothing has crawled up mine and died!" I say abruptly and am secretly chuffed with the speed of my wit. With this Little Miss Happy openly explodes into loud cries of laughter, as do half of the carriage and finally the train doors spring open. I practically throw myself out of them to escape and inhale the fresh air just as I can hear a claps of appreciation coming from the carriage. As I pass, I smile and dutifully bow my head in acceptance and can already see the funny side. *Well that was a different journey than I had foreseen!*

"Feckin bastards." I hear Mr Smelly curse as he waddles off. *What a complete looser!*

I continue to walk briskly along the platform, out of the station and along the road to ensure that he can't catch me up. As I go I dodge the triple drains and only treading on the double ones, in the hope that this will increase the chances of my day getting better. *Three are unlucky, whereas two are good luck.. although in all honesty I have no idea why.*

I arrive on time, the meeting goes well and later that day whilst on my journey home, I'm pleased to hear from the client that they would like my input on this project. *Oh good, this will keep some money coming in and lessen the guilt of writing my book a little.*

So for the next few days my book takes a bit of a back seat, as I plough my time and energy into designs, quotations, presentations etc. and it's not until Friday that I manage to find the time to squeeze in some writing. Instantly my imagination is alive again, stories fill my head and I'm off on a tangent, tapping away at my keypad for hours on end, not even stopping for lunch. By chance, I glance up at the clock just in the nick of time, I have approximately ten minutes before I have to pick the kids up from school. I race to my car in a panic as I realise that I will now have to park at least a ten minute walk away because it will be heaving and so by the time I reach the boys, they will unsurprisingly have the hump with me.

As I fight my way through the stream of parents and children all vacating the premises in the opposite direction to us, I see Lloyd waiting patiently in the playground and gesture at him to run around to Johns classroom. We make it there totally breathless, just as his teacher is closing the doors for the day and I apologise for holding her up. We all then continue our sprint around the now empty building, to Henrys classroom and by the time we get there I can barely breath, let alone speak.

We burst in through the double doors like a whirlwind and begin making our apology's for the second time in the last five minutes but I'm noticing a bit of tension. I put it down to our lateness on a Friday afternoon, when everyone wants to get home nice and early to begin their weekend. That is, until I look around the spotless room, to where Henry is sitting, legs crossed, eyes down. *Oh shit, what's he done?* And here it comes..

"Hello Mrs Gooden, can I have a quick word please." Asks his teacher and I wonder what she'd say if I were to say 'no'? I glance back over to Henry who still hasn't dared to look up and I notice that his lip is now quivering too. *It must be bad.*
"Unfortunately we've had a bit of an incident with Henry today." She begins and I try desperately to listen *and* compose my breathing simultaneously, so that I can deal with this in a professional manner.
"Oh okay" I pant. *And breathe!*
"What's happened?" I continue whilst desperately trying swallow, to curb the panting.
"Well I'm afraid that he and another child were fighting over a toy this afternoon...." I've zoned out and am only half listening now, as my mind flashes back to Monday morning and how I was made late because I had to speak with her about the group of boys that were fighting.
"Oh god, not the bloody train thing?!" I suddenly blurt out, rudely interrupting her with no thought for my language. *I have to say that I will be slightly miffed if it is.*
"The train crossing sign. Yes that's right." She confirms, nodding her head and I let out an involuntarily tut and I feel my cheeks instantly redden.
"Look, I'm not being funny okay but I did mention the other day that it was causing a lot of friction between Henry and a few of the other boys, who were all fighting over it and suggested that it was put away in case there were causalities. It was rather large and looked heavy too, I suspect it could cause quite a blow". I say trying to get in early to argue his case, whilst still struggling to breath.
"That may be true." She says and her expression tells me that I haven't helped the situation at all and in fact may have just made her slightly mad.
"But if we stopped the children from playing with all of the toys that they argued over, we would have quite an empty nursery." She continued, all high and mighty and I could feel myself getting cross now too.

"Yes, I realise that.." I start but it is now her turn to interrupt me.

"In this instance Mrs Gooden, the child had to be collected early and taken to the hospital, as he has a deep wound on his forehead." *Bollocks! What is it with trains this week?*

"Oh." I say now, not only feeling silly for arguing with her but also in total shock at what Henry has done.

"As you can imagine, the Mother was none too pleased." *Oh great, that hadn't even crossed my mind! Monday morning is going to be fun... NOT!!!*

"Don't worry, I'll be having words with Henry over the weekend and have him make a 'sorry' card for the other child." I try to make a plan to support her.

"That would be good, thank you. But you do realise that we cannot tolerate this kind of behaviour." She says. *God he's three, I'm sure it wasn't his intention to hospitalise a child!*

"Yes I know. As I said before, I will be speaking to him about what happened today." I say, feeling now that it is my mothering skills that are being questioned with no mention about where the members of staff all were whilst this was all going on?!

"Who is it that he hit by the way?" I ask hopefully, knowing that she is not permitted to tell me.

"We're not allowed to say." She replies and practically closes the door in our faces.

"Oh right." I say back to the door. *Rude!* If only I could gag that child until he forgets which boy hurt him.

Everyone will know on Monday morning... let's just hope the Mum isn't one of the rough ones!!

All of the way home I shout at Henry whilst the other two sit in complete silence, knowing that there's a possibility that they could get a mouthful too if they make a sound.

When Dick gets in, I update him and he too scolds Henry and tells him that he'll have to go to bed without dinner. I can almost see him rubbing his hands together with the money that that'll save, being as it's curry night! *This time last week it was John that missed out and so he is looking quite smug with himself now.* Later that night I call Mum, I can always rely on her to make me feel better about any situation and as predicted, she's in agreement with me, they should have been being watched more closely.

"For god sake, he's three!" Her words echo my own thoughts.

"I know. I mean, I know he's in the wrong but I could see it coming a mile off!" I tell her and explain the scene from Monday morning.

"Well, if you had already warned them on Monday and they didn't listen then that's not poor Henrys fault, it's theirs!" She says, sticking up for Henry as I knew she would.

"You should go to the head!" She continues and we eventually agree that it's best to leave it, rather than gaining him a reputation right at the start of his educational journey and instead we joke about beating the teacher over the head with the bloody toy!

Saturday morning after the boys have cleared their homework and John has made his card, we choose our lottery numbers in the same way as usual. I choose: '2' Being the number of arguments that I have had with complete strangers recently. '27' as that's today's dates, and tonight WILL be the day we win the lottery and '59' to beat Dick to it and I can see out of the corner of my eye that this has annoyed him slightly, he will now have to come up with a new method of choosing.

After a little thought, Dicks choices this week are: '40', '45' and '49' because he believes that the reason we don't ever win anything is because our number choices are generally low and spaced out too much. *I'm not convinced that that makes the blindest bit of difference myself but hey hoo!*

Lloyd's attention is back with us this week and he has decided on: '2 'and '5' as he has learnt that these are the only prime numbers that can end with a '2' or a '5'... at which point I had actually switched off?! And '31' the date of Wednesdays draw and our second chance if we don't win tonight.

John isn't sulking this week and so opts for: '5' as he hasn't had his name moved again at school all week, '7' the age of his new and very grown up 'girl buddy' from along the road and '50', Daddy's age. At which point Dick chases him around the house and tells him not to be so cheeky.

I merge Henrys two most used numbers this week to '37'. So, after a bit of disagreement with Dick about how the numbers are arranged, everyone is happy and in agreement and this week's lottery numbers are as follows + one lucky dip:

Line One: 2, 5, 7, 27, 31 and 37.

Line Two: 37, 40, 45, 49, 50 and 59.

11

The second half can only get better!

Today is 'day one' of the half term.   I lie in bed pretending
to be dead every time that one of the boys peer their heads
around the door and whispers out to me 'Mum... are you
awake'.   *Just let me enjoy not having to rush around like a maniac for
a few seconds more, please!*   But by around nine thirtyish I give
in and get up, feeling reasonable well rested.   Up until this
point Lloyd had been lying on his bed both playing on the
iPad and watching the telly I suspect, by how quiet he has
been.   The other two are in their room, watching exactly the
same programmes as Lloyd.   *I know this because their TV's are
slightly out of sync with each other which is quite annoying to listen to.*
I stick my toes out of the duvet and am about to get up
when the Spud starts to meow really loudly.   I stroke her in
attempt to shut her up but even over the sound of their TV's
the boys have clocked my movement and suddenly they all
descend on my room, like little magnets.
John is dressed already and has a baseball cap on with his
earphones over the top, which he has plugged into his
electric guitar and is strumming away, whilst checking out his
reflection in our mirrored wardrobes.   Henry is on the
keyboard also wearing a cap, naked as always and singing at
high level, whilst Lloyd is talking over them both, trying to
explain to me how far he has got on his new game and I try
to look as interested as I can be in all of them, given the fact
that I have just woken up.

Okay breakfast time, me thinks! I tie my hair back and then order everyone to make their beds before going downstairs if they want breakfast.

Mental note - To let them have a really late night tonight and hopefully get a bit of a lie in tomorrow morning.

As I flattened my own sheets I can feel that they are wet. *Calf boy obviously hasn't taken his night nappy off again and it's leaked everywhere arh!* I strip the sheets from the bed, throw them into one of the many washing baskets that we have dotted around the house, some full of clean clothes, some full of ironing still to be done but this particular one is currently already half full with dirty clothes. I then go to check that everyone else's beds aren't wet too because there would be no way that the boys would notice this until they pull back their sheets tonight. Henry's is soaking, so I remove his sheets too realising that I already have at least three loads of washing to do. Downstairs I load the first lot into the washing machine and start making breakfasts. As it's the holidays and as regular as clockwork, Lloyd has asked for a 'BS' and the younger two both want beans on toast. *It's like ground hog day in this house!*
I have arranged lots of outside activities for this week, to try to keep the kids entertained and avoid as many arguments as possible. *After the last break when I considered driving them all somewhere and leaving them there. I think the following Monday morning was the earliest we had ever arrived at school and I nearly skipped out after dropping them all off!* Today is their only day indoors, as I need to work. I tell them to choose a film and get the blankets out and explain that later on I have a drawing competition for them to enter, to try to win us all a holiday but only if they behave in the mean time.

I then make a drink for each and snuggle them into separate areas of the lounge, out of touching distance of each other, to avoid little niggles and for approximately an hour it works. In which time I have only made half of the phone calls that I need to and know that I can make no more for a while because any minute now one of them will be in to tell tales on the others, as I can hear the tension building.

John has got out of his seat and moved across to Henry's seat and as he has lifts the cover to climb under, Henry pulls it away from him.

"Go away, it's mine." He screams.

"I want to cuddle you." John replies sweetly in a tone meant to sound like a baby.

"Oh come on then, you can sit here." Henry says, tapping the seat next to him but within minutes the niceties have gone and they are punching each other. *Any minute now, Henry will be in in tears.*

"Mummy! Mummy! Mummy, John hurt me!" Henry cries as he approaches the office door but there are no tears and so I know it's not serious.

"Just move away from him then." I say turning back to my computer, trying to sort the issue without having to stop working and off he toddles back into the front room.

"John leave him alone!" I call out, so that he has been warned.

Ten minutes later John asks "Mum, can I play on the iPad please?"

"Yes of course you can darling, you know where it is." I reply, unaware of the mayhem that will follow.

Suddenly I hear an almighty shrill. I quickly get up to see what's going on, worried that someone could be seriously hurt. As I enter I see Lloyd stood up, holding the iPad in one hand above his head, his other arm is stretched out holding Johns head away from him, as John tries to punch and kick him, to no prevail.

"What the hell is going on!?" I yell, still shocked by the initial outburst but it doesn't take much imagination to figure it out.

"I was just sitting here, minding my own business and John came over and tried to snatch the iPad off of me. Why does he always try to wind me up?!" Lloyd explains, still in his awkward pose.

"You said that I could have a go, didn't you Mummy." John says, expecting me to back him up and trying to act innocent.

"You're right, I did." I confirm. "But I didn't realise that Lloyd was already using it, you really shouldn't snatch it's not nice!" I reprimand him and with that he's in tears but these tears don't accompany a sorry face, instead he is angry!

"Right, let Lloyd finish the game that he is on and then it's your turn." I say, smiling at John and hoping that it's contagious before turning to Lloyd.

"Lloyd finish what you are doing and then let John have it for a while please. You're always on it, he doesn't ask very often."

"What! That is so unfair" He shrills at me. "He's mean and you're still taking his side." *Oh woe is me!*

"No I'm not taking any sides thank you and if you back chat me anymore, you won't even finish the game that you're on." I say, trying to be the adult.

"Come on, be reasonable, after half an hour you can have it back and so on, you have to take turns." I finish and believing the ordeal to be over, turn to leave the room. Just as I do though, John tries to make Henry his allie and Henry just loves this!

"Lloyds such a baby isn't he Henry?" He whispers, loud enough for us all to hear.

"Yeah, he's a baby. He's not my best friend. You're my best friend John. We don't like him do we?!" Henry joins in with the taunts.

"No we don't, he's a meanie." John continues, trying to goad Lloyd into another fight.

I glance over at Lloyd now to gage his expression and Johns plan has worked, I can see the anger building in his face. He glares at John with raged eyes, puts down the iPad and makes a running attack on him as John runs away and after a bit of a chase, a full scale fight erupts. I shout at them both to stop but have to physically separate them because they have blocked my voice out. *Great, now I'm mad too!* I make both of them sit down, take the iPad out to the kitchen and place it on the side before taking a deep breath and returning to the lounge.

"Right, now neither of you can have it!" I say, still in a raised tone.

"Didn't want it anyway." Mumbles John.

"Sorry?" I question him but he doesn't dare repeat what he's said.

"Don't push your luck John." I say, trying to keep calm.

"Why did you take it off of me then and start all of this, if you don't want it anyway?" If you hadn't snatched it, we wouldn't have argued in the first place." He sensibly points out, in a now screechy voice and I can tell that he's on the verge of tears.

"Alright everyone, now drop it and watch the rest of the film. I don't want to hear another word! If you haven't got anything nice to say, don't bother saying anything at all! Just ignore each other." I say and turn once again to leave.

"I'm not listening!" John says. *Why does he always have to have the last bloody word, it's infuriating!*

"Oh dear, here we go.... Johns getting into one of his 'moods' again Mummy! You're so moody, I'm surprised you have any friends." Lloyd says, trying to act grown up. *Oh god, here we go again!*

"I'm not in a mood and anyway it's your fault!" He yells back at him, getting really angry now and his face is bright red.

"I'm not listening! I'm not listening!" Retaliates Lloyd.

"You're a big baby and a big fat liar!" John shouts at him.

"I'm not listening, I'm not listening." Lloyd taunts him again.

"BELT UP!!!" I scream over the pair of them.

"Close your mouth coz I don't even want to breathe the same air as you." Lloyd continues, covering his own mouth and nose with his blanket as Henry moves closer to him and practically coughs in his face.

"Right, that's it!" I continue as I feel myself starting to lose the plot slightly, knowing that another fight is about to kick off.

"I'm not listening, I'm not listening." Starts John this time and I can't figure out whether he's talking to Lloyd or to me?

"John, you go to your room and Lloyd you go to yours. You can both stay up there until I tell you to come down. If you're going to be horrible to each other, I don't want to hear it. What a great start to the holidays hey?!" I state firmly, as I prepare myself for possibly of having to carry John upstairs because, as Lloyd pointed out he is now fully having one of his 'moods' and so, forth coming stubbornness is inevitable.

Lloyd springs up instantly and leaves the room, apologising and telling me that he will try harder as he goes.   John though, doesn't shift in inch.   Instead, he stares down at his toes occasionally peering up at me without moving his head, with a look on his face like I'm about to beat him.

"I said, go up to your room John." I repeat myself sternly.

"No. I won't." He mumbles.

"Yes. You will." I tell him slowly, trying not to raise my voice whilst staring at him in my best authoritive way, all the while knowing that I am now the target for his 'mood'. *I will have to see this through now otherwise he will claim it as a victory and we will be back to square one with future episodes.*

"No. I won't." He repeats himself without raising his head.

"Don't make me carry you up!" I warn him, still remaining as calm as I can. *I need to be in control of this!* "You know why you need to go upstairs and have some time alone don't you, we've spoken about this lots of times, it helps everyone to calm down and remember how to be nice to each other."

"Lloyd's gone now and so I'll be good now! It's all his fault." He says, trying to strike up his own deal so that I'll back down.

"I've made him have time out, just as I'm making you. So you need to do the same please, otherwise it's not fair." I tell him.

"It's not fair!" He protests, wavy his arms around at me.

"It is totally fair John." I say bluntly back. "What wouldn't be fair, would be if I let you stay down here and argue with me, when Lloyd has done exactly what I have asked of him and straight away, with no fuss." With this, he gets up, pushes past me and stamps up the stairs, shouting out but not daring to look at me.

"You are a horrible lady! You are not a good Mummy!" *Yeah, cheers!*

And again I'm mad, actually worse than mad, I'm livid but I don't let him witness this nor do I answer him, I just return to the front room and turn on Peppa Pig for the now ever so quiet, Henry. Whose little face lights up instantly and he speaks.

"Who's being the best behaved Mummy?" *You've got to love his cheek.*

"You have. By far, my darling." I say and his grin grows even more.

Mental Note - To check to see whether anyone is using the iPad in future before agreeing to anything!

As I sit back down in my office I can hear John slamming doors and banging around upstairs and have to stop myself from going up to tell him off some more. I'm still too mad to confront him. *I wonder exactly how you're supposed to deal with this sort of behaviour?* Within ten minutes though the banging has subsided and is replaced instead with a deadly silence. I go up and check on both of the boys, in case the banging was actually them signalling to me for help (which I had just ignored). Lloyd is playing with his Lego and asks if I'm okay and whether he can come downstairs now, as he has learnt his lesson. I tell him that he can, but that he needs to make up with John first and then lecture him about how brothers should stick together, as they will be friends for life *(PMA)!*

But when I go to find John he's asleep just inside the entrance to his bedroom, the rage has obviously taken its toll and zapped him of all of his energy. I lift him up and carry him over to his bed, where I gently place him down. I sit for a while and admire his gorgeous little face. He's such a lovely boy ninety nine percent of the time, he's so loving, so caring, it makes me sad that he gets into states like this. I so hope that he grows out of it soon. I know that when he wakes up, he will be cross with himself and will shadow me for the rest of the day to try to make it up to me and that I'll forgive him straight away because he tries so hard. And I'm right, about an hour later as I sit typing away on my laptop, I hear him quietly enter the office. I don't turn around and instead let him take his own time. From behind he wraps his little arms around my neck and he whispers in my ear.

"I'm so sorry Mummy. I do try to be good. My brain just forgets sometimes." This statement brings a tear to my eye, I know he tries, bless him. He's forgiven. *How could anyone stay mad at him now?*

I call it a day with my work, it's impossible to get on with everything with them all here. Instead I summands everyone to the dinner table and get out some card and the 'creative' box. Pens and pencils can be used at any time in our house but *strictly* in the dining room only *(this rule was implicated after Lloyd drew all over my Mums wallpaper once, when he was left unsupervised at her house)* . The 'creative' box however only comes out when I am around to monitor the mess. *Glitter can take months to tidy up once it's be thrown everywhere!* I read the rules of the competition out loud to all three of them, as my mind races around the word 'prize' and I am far more excited about this than they are.

"Each applicant should be under the age of 10." I say and then stop and to look around them. "Oh what a shame Lloyd, you're too old."

"No I'm not, I'm eight?" He says confused.

"Oh yes, sorry my mistake! I thought you were seventy eight." I say and smile at him, as he rolls his eyes and shakes his head at me.

"One lucky winner will enjoy a family holiday to Walt Disney World, Orlando for fourteen nights, flying enhanced economy flights with Virgin Atlantic, park tickets and.." With this all three join me in excitement and are already planning what they are going to do/see etc. *Oh dear, maybe I've built it up too much!* I skip the finer details and carry on with the rules.

"Right... how to enter." I say scanning the page, to cut out what they don't need to hear.

"To be in with a chance of winning, using an A4 sheet of card your child should design their own form on transport, to travel on their holiday in and write a short note describing what their invention can do." I continue, not looking up.

"Oohh that's so hard!" Moans Lloyd, defeated already.

We lovingly refer to Lloyd as 'Emmet' (from the Lego Movie) on occasions such as this, Emmet is so used to working to a plan, that he has forgotten how to create and this sums Lloyd up!

"Oh come on Emmet, dig deep!" I smile at him who tries not to smile back but can't help himself as Henry begins calling the register loudly. *He obviously didn't get the rules!* "Oh this is easy." Says John, who is already scribbling away and the roles of power are temporarily reversed and Lloyd studies Johns work, in total ore of his creative skills.

After a few minutes John jumps down and turns on some rock music (something he likes to do to help him to stay focused), which we're all pleased about as it also serves the purpose of drowning out Henry, who is again calling the register. And at last, they are all calm and too busy in their own thoughts to annoy each other. I make myself a cup of tea, sit back and watch them working whilst thinking how, with lots of plans made, the second half can only get better!!

12

Well I never!

Late Tuesday evening as I bath the children after a day in the park, the phone rings.   It's Rose, she has called to see whether I would like her and Frank to take the boys out for the day tomorrow.   There's an event on at a local tourist attraction and they have a year's passes, so thought the boys may enjoy it.   I tell her that they would love to go, we were only going swimming anyway and make this an excuse for them all to have an early night.

"Nanny won't want to take out grumpy children."   I tell them all.

"Oh but it's the holidays."   Protests Lloyd.

"I know but it is okay you know to have at least one early night."   I tell him as I pat his hair dry because otherwise it would be left dripping on to his pyjamas, where he wouldn't even think to do it himself.

"I don't ever get grumpy."   He says and he's right, he's always slow but very rarely moody.

"I know."   I say, as I wink at him and he knows instantly that this means we are now humouring the younger two boys and allowing him a little longer but want to avoid protest from them too.

"Okay, I'll have an early night."   He says, in a winey voice acting way too obvious but neither of the other two boys recognise or question this and although I do make him go up slightly earlier than usual, I let him read for as long as he wants in bed, knowing that his eyes will defeat him within half an hour anyway.

The next morning Rose and Frank arrive just after ten and although the boys are dressed, have eaten and brushed their teeth, they are all still pruning their hairstyles in the mirror. I tell them to hurry up and when they finally emerge from the bathroom, I joke that I'm glad that they are not coming out with me with those hairstyles (even though they all look gorgeous as always). Rose laughs as she herds them outside and into Franks car while suggesting a plan.

"We'll go for a pizza after, to give you some more time to work if you like?"

"Or Subway?!" Lloyd interrupts excitedly as he stops getting into the car and instead turns around, giving us the biggest (hopeful) grin.

"We'll take a vote on it later on." Rose says diplomatically.

"Oh cheers, you're a star!" I say, thankful of at least one day of peace this week to finish the work that I should have done yesterday.

"Do we need to be home by a certain time?" She asks as she gets into the car.

"No. See ya tomorrow." I laugh and hear the boys reprimand me from the back of the car.

"Bye!" They all yell out to me and me to them.

And with that they are off, waving at me as they go and I'm taken back to how my Mum used to worry about me and my sisters when we all went out in the car together with my Nan and Grandad.

I work all day and from my office window, watch Franks car pull into the driveway at around six thirty. *Peace is shattered!* Within seconds of the boys getting out of the car, the house is filled with bells ringing, doors banging and lots of shouting. They excitedly tell me stories about looking around submarines, seeing boats, studying the detailed model ships and each of them has made a piece of rope in the ropery.

One by one they each dangle these in front of my face, until I go a bit cross-eyed. I admire their work and tell them how clever they all are. They have obviously all had a good day! They go on to describe what pizzas they ate and which of their friends they bumped into.

Rose and Frank stay for a drink and then joke about having to go home and sit in a darkened room, with a glass of wine, in peace for the rest of the evening before quickly reassuring me that all three have behaved immaculately all day. *I'm not so sure that I believe that!* And by eight o'clock all three are soundo on the sofa, so me and Dick carry them up to bed. The next morning we were due to meet a few other Mums at a local farm but I call around each and arrange to meet instead at a local indoor play centre because it's absolutely chucking it down outside and I don't fancy being cold and wet all day. *Not only that, I could only imagine the state of the car afterwards, I still haven't got around to cleaning it out much to Mum's frustration.* At the ripe old age of eight, Lloyd considers himself 'too old' for indoor play centres but even he likes this particular one as, along with the usual soft play area and restaurant, it also has high ropes that span the majority of the ceiling. This is right up his street, he's a bit of a thrill seeker. A few years ago, during a long weekend in Centre Parks, he was the smallest child there to take part in the adults 'Tree top challenge', which saw him climb thirty foot high trees and zip wire across the half of the length of the pond, much to the surprise of all of the adults participating (and us) who made such a fuss of him for being so brave. For once, we arrive on time and as we stand at the high level counter that only Lloyd is tall enough to see over *(even though the other two try their hardest on tiptoe to no avail),* he spots some of his friends and is already removing his shoes, with the others following suit as they can sense his excitement. I try to make a plan in advance..

"Leave your socks on please and don't disappear until you have seen where I'm sitting. Then you'll know where to find us, in case anyone gets hurt or lost." I say quickly but it falls on deaf ears.

"And I need to know what you want to eat too please..." But as soon as I hand over the money and the lady behind the counter pushes the switch, allowing the entrance gate that was locking us out, to swing open of its own accord and let us in, they're gone, just like that! Totally ignoring my instructions and I instantly lose sight of all three at the same time. I peer down at the floor and all that is left behind is a pile of coats and shoes, which I bend down and scoop up. I then systematically drop a shoe every three paces and then pick it up again to drop another, whilst at the same time searching the space for the other Mums, secretly hoping that I'm the first to arrive. *Bloody kids!* I'm not. Instead, I am as usual the last. I approach the group, we all say our hello's and everyone shuffles around to pass me a chair. As I take one and sit down, I open my arms allowing all of the coats and shoes to fall out and form a new pile on the floor and the other Mums help to kick the shoes safely under the table with the others and throw the coats onto the pile.

Mental note - To try to be the first to arrive at least once in my life - on this occasion I was on time but to be the first I NEED to leave the house earlier!

As usual we begin chatting instantly about how the kids are getting on at school, their teachers, the other Mums etc. and within minutes of arriving, the older ones have grouped up and are already in their harnesses, climbing the ramp up to the high ropes above our heads.

They occasionally call down to us to watch how good they are at the different activities. Whist the smaller children have totally disappeared from sight into the maze of other kids, soft play and fun, looking for familiar faces. Every now and then come back to tell us tales or for a toilet break or for us to kiss their wounds but as fast as they come, they are gone again. Everyone is happy.

It's only after about half an hour of chatting that I realise that I haven't even had a cup of tea yet. I ask around the group to see whether anyone else would like anything while I'm there and then join the long queue, all waiting to be served by the one poor member of staff on today. With all of our chatting, I hadn't realised how busy it was here today! I wait patiently, looking around to see if I can catch sight of any of my children so that I can order their lunches now, to save queuing up again later but they are nowhere to be seen. I daren't decide for them, I would only get it wrong. Not only that, I'd have to search the entire centre to find them all when the food arrives if I hadn't pre-warned them to come back to the table.

Mental note - To get their orders during the car journey in future!

I stare up at the chalked menu behind the counter and realise that I am really hungry! I read through the endless choices and my stomach rumbles like mad. Just as I'm making deciding between a baguette or a toasted sandwich in my head, John bounds into me all sweaty and red faced, making me momentarily lose my footing.

"Careful!" I scold him as I stand straight again, jabbing him in the ribs to show that I'm just joking.

"Can I have a drink please Mum, I'm absolutely boiling?" He asks, running his fingers through his wet hair and smiling up at me. *God he's cute!*

"Yes of course, water?" I ask and continue before he can answer and disappear again.

"Can you quickly go and find the others and see what they want to eat please, then come straight back." I ask him, emphasising the words 'straight back'.

"The options are nuggets, burger or fish fingers." I tell him.

"Yeah okay. Yes water please." He replies and runs off, in the direction of where he left the others and I'm left wondering whether I'll see him again before I reach the counter.

Five minutes pass and he's back "Me and Henry will have a jacket potato with cheese and beans and Lloyd wants a tuna sandwich, with salt and vinegar crisps, raisins and a Coke."

Good old Lloyd, as specific as ever... well that buggers tonight's dinner up then but it's that or I go looking for them myself and I really can't be arsed!

"I don't remember any of those being in the list I gave you?" I laugh and he grins too.

"You and Henry are going to look like baked beans soon! Can you tell everyone that I want them back at the table in ten minutes please or I'll be mad and you don't wanna see me mad!" I joke.

"Okedokie. Where's my water?"

"Erm..." I say, pulling the neck of my collar away and peering into my jumper "It's not there?"

"Hhhmmm... where is it?" He says again rolling his eyes at me.

"I haven't been served yet darling. Go and get three bottles of water out of the fridge please, I'm next." He goes off and comes back with two bottles of water and a Capri Sun and I shake my head at him.

"You'll have to change the others too if you're not having water. Change Lloyds for a Coke and Henry's for a Capri Sun too please, otherwise there will be arguments." I instruct him.

"Okay." He says and does as I ask.

While I'm being served John disappears with the drinks to give to the others and I try to call after him for them to drink it up at the table but he doesn't hear me. I pay and as I turn to walk back to the table, I trip up on a handbag that has been left on the floor behind me, right by me feet sending my coffee flying.

"Oh god, sorry!!!' I say, although I'm not sure why I am apologising.. I didn't leave it there! I try to compose myself and when I look up I instantly recognise the lady... its Annabelle.

"No it's my fault sorry, my bloody bag's like a suitcase it's always getting in the way! I shouldn't have left it there." She says and then makes eye contact.

"My bags the same, don't worry." I assure her.

"Oh hello!" She says, smiling at me.

"We meet again." I say. *God this is just weird, how many times can you bump into someone?!*

"You really aren't good with hot beverages are you?!" She laughs and I'm instantly drawn back to shitty trouser stains and feel slightly embarrassed all over again.

Mental note - To stop apologising for things that aren't my fault!

"I'll get you another. What would you like?" She asks, nodding at my half empty cup.

"Oh cheers, that was a white coffee I'll have the same again please." I say politely.

"No worries." She says and then tells the young man behind the counter her entire order, while I stand beside her feeling awkward.

"So, you have kids then?" She asks. "I have only ever seen you alone."

I wonder what she's actually thinking with that statement. Does she think that I palm my kids off? She doesn't even know me.

"Yes, three boys. I take it that you do too and that you aren't here just for the fun of it?" I laugh whilst making an underlying point that I've never seen her with her kids either.

"Really, I have three boys too." She says, obviously surprised that there are two people in the world mad enough to have carried on procreating after two children. *Well I never!*

"Charlie, Jack and Harry. Charlie's eight, Jack's six and Harry's five." She continues proudly.

"Oh my goodness, they are *really* close in age to my boys. How funny." I say as I wonder how she always manages to look so well turned out and I don't?

"Lloyd is eight, John's six and Henry's three." I say and as I do so am aware that I sound as proud as she did to inform her of this.

"What school do they go to?"

"Fairchoice." She says, as she hands me a new coffee and I thank her with a smile.

"Oh wow, so do mine! They *must* know each other!" I say and as I do so catch sight of Lloyd talking to a boy that I don't recognise.

"Well, what a small world! They only started there this term and so they may not know each other but they seem to really enjoy it there so far." She says and she too is looking in Lloyds direction.

"There's my eldest over there." She says pointing out the boy next to Lloyd.

"Wow and that's my eldest with him." I laugh and we look at each other with amusement and it's quite clear that we both instantly feel much more relaxed with each other now.

"Are you here alone?" I ask looking around.

"Yes, do you want to join me?" She asks kindly.

"Well, I am actually here with some of the Mums. Why don't you join us? They are all really nice." I ask pointing over to our table and for the first time since meeting this lady I really do want to get to know her better.

"Erm.. yeah okay then. I'll be over in a bit if that's okay?"

"Yeah of course." I reassure her as I can tell that I have given her little choice.

I return to the others and notice a clear table next to ours and so quickly shove a load of shoes underneath it and hang some coats over the chairs, so that the kids will have somewhere to eat their lunches when they return. I pull two of the seats out, angling them towards the others and sit on one, so that Annabelle won't have the awkwardness of having to sit besides someone that she has never met when she does join us.

"My friend Annabelle will be over in a minute." I inform the others in case they wonder who the hell she is and nod my head in Annabelle's direction. "Her kids have just started at Fairchoice, so I thought it would be nice if she joins us, if that's okay with you guys?"

"That's fine with me honey, the more the merrier." Smiles Penny in between conversations.

Penny is one of my favourite school 'Mum's'. She has a cute little boy called 'Paul' who is in John's year but not his class. She is slightly older than the rest of our little group but you would never know it, she is very attractive and her social life is better than mine was at eighteen - you have to literally book her in weeks in advance for anything. She has a kind face, which mimics her personality and we often enjoy a good catch up over a glass or two of wine. Sometimes with her husband joins us too, he's equally as lovely and likes to be up to date on all of the gossip.

"Same as!" Laughs Suzy before adding. "But if she turns out to be a physco, she's all yours! My life's hectic enough." Suzy is another of my favourite 'Mum's'. She has a naturally funny sense of humour that shows in her facial expressions. Since the day we met, she's always lovingly referred to me as 'E' and it makes me smile every time I hear it. Up until two years ago Suzy had just the one little boy 'Albert', a cheeky little fella who is one of Lloyds close friends and then two years ago she had her second and has since had her third, so her life has changed quite a bit. Her life is now like my own, one big rush but she's always happy and upbeat even when she's knackered.

All of the others are too busy talking and so I don't interrupt, I know that Suzy or Penny will quietly fill in the gaps should they question who she is. Annabelle joins us about ten minutes later and as I watch her approach us, she reminds me of myself a bit, although a younger version. She has three pairs of shoes in her arms, some of which have dropped to the floor and so she is kicking them along in front of her, a bag over her shoulders and four coats stuffed under her arm. I reach out and help her with the coats and she smiles.

"Bloody kids!" She says as she sits down, dumping the rest of the shoes under the table. "I found one of the kids 'Charlie' and asked him to go and get the others so that they could help me over her with all of this bloody gear but after sitting there waiting like a complete twat, can you believe not one of them came back! I bet you thought I was a right rude bitch!?"

"No, don't be silly!" I reassure her and begin to introduce her to the others. "Everyone, this is Annabelle."

"Yeah you may have heard about Eva's strange stalker lady, that's me." She laughs and I feel slightly guilty that I actually have spoken about her to Penny and Suzy but know that they wouldn't mention anything.

"Oh don't be silly." With this I can see some of the women look at me as if to say 'why do we not know this story', so I brush it off and quickly continue to work my way around the group, introducing each as I go. "She has recently moved to Rainham and her kids go to Fairchoice too now. Annabelle, this is Penny, this is Suzy, this is..."

Two minutes later all six boys appear at the table and Lloyd excitedly announces "Mummy, meet the 'Bailey Brothers'."

"This is Charlie, he's in my class. This is Jack, he's in Johns year and this little cutie, is Harry." He says, affectionately playing with Harrys cheeks.

"And this is their Mummy, Annabelle." I state just as confidentially, gesturing to Annabella and it takes him aback.

"I didn't know that you knew Charlie's Mum, Mum?" He questions me and I can tell that he's rather put out that I hadn't shared this information before.

"Well, we only met recently." I update him and roll my eyes at his indignant stare.

"Oh. Can Charlie and his brothers come to ours after? Charlie loves Pokémon like me and I want to show him my cards *and* what I've built in Minecraft!" He wines, holding his hands in a praying position as he pleads with me.

"Not today gorgeous but they can another day." I say, giving him the 'don't ask again or you'll be in trouble' look.

"Oh p-l-e-a-s-e!!!" Moans Charlie to Annabelle now.

"Not today Charlie. By the time we get back from here you'll be shattered and we've got Nanny and Granddad coming over tonight too. They would be very disappointed if they couldn't see you." She backs me up and with that thankfully their lunches arrive, so the conversation is dropped fairly quickly.

As we start talking, it's as though me and Annabelle have been friends for years. We talk mainly about our kids and their weird little habits, about the school and it's clubs, about where we live and her new home and before we know it all of the other Mums are calling their children back to the table and are preparing to leave. I make my apologies to everyone for not having spoken to them much but they don't mind and in all honesty, I am not at all sorry because I have really enjoyed my afternoon getting to know Annabelle.

"I suppose we had better go home too." I say as I look around again for my children, who are as standard nowhere to be seen and notice that it is practically empty.

"Yeah, us too. Mikes Mum and Dad are coming over in an hour and I need to do a quick run around 'clean' before they arrive. My house looks like a bloody bomb has hit it!" She says laughing and I know that feeling only too well.

"I'll be glad when the kids go back to bloody school and I can get straight again." She continues.

"I know exactly what you mean." I laugh and we gather our children together and make our way out to the car park.

"I work at the coffee shop most week days, pop in for a cuppa and a chat next time you're passing, it'll be lovely to see you." She says and then hands me a scrap of paper. "Here's my phone number."

"Oh cheers, I'll text you mine." I say honestly, knowing that I will because she has been really good company.

"Cool." She pauses, before saying sweetly. "Listen, thank you for a lovely afternoon! I don't know many people yet, so it's really kind of you to introduce me to all of your friends."

"Don't be silly, it's been lovely." I say honestly, as I feel a little glow inside. *That's my good deed done for the day!*

"I absolutely hate coming to these places don't you? I only came today because the kids were all doing my head in and it was pissing it down outside. I'm really glad I did now." She thanks me once again.

"Me too!" I agree. "It's funny to think that I've been actively trying to avoid you for the last few weeks and now we are friends, isn't it."

"Oh... have you?" She asks, looking slightly hurt and I instantly regret my admission. *Oh bollocks, I've upset her!*

"Well no, no, not avoiding you exactly." I stutter, trying to back track whilst feeling my cheeks heat up as I struggle with what I am trying to say. "Well yeah, kind of avoiding you but... but only because I'm trying to write a book and.... Look it's a long story, why don't we all meet up tomorrow and I'll tell you all about it."

As the words fall out of my mouth, I realise that I should have checked that she was free before mentioning this in front of the kids because now, all six boys are jumping around like nutters, screaming with excitement and so she will really be in the dog house if she says no.

"Sorry! Me and my big mouth. Are you about tomorrow?" " I say quickly, covering my mouth with my hand.

"Actually we aren't doing anything, so that'll be lovely." She confirms. I'm pleased and the boys are elated.

"It may just save me killing one of my children too!" She laughs, giving all of the children a playful look before confirming the details. "Where shall we meet?"

"Do you want to come to mine? The weather's supposed to be horrible again and so the kids can just hang out together." I suggest, picturing in my head that mayhem to follow.

"It's a date! Is after lunch okay with you, I've got a few things to do first?" Annabelle asks and I'm secretly pleased to not be making lunch for anyone as my children have eaten us out of house and home this week and that would mean a trip to the shops to restock. Something that I always try to avoid when Henry is with me, as it usually ends up with me dragging him back to the car following a massive meltdown after I have told him that he can't have something.

"Lovely. I'll text you our address now." I say and promptly begin tapping away at my phone.

"Cool, we will see you tomorrow then." She says brightly and I am happy to see that she is no longer offended by my stupid, ill thought out comment.

Mental note - To think before I speak!

The boys chase each other around the car park, hug and wave goodbye and everyone leaves happy, safe in the knowledge that they will be together again tomorrow. Our entire journey home is filled with the boys excited talk about what toys they will show the 'Bailey Brothers' tomorrow. When we reach home Dick is in already and as I enter the kitchen I find him kneeling down, staring into the fridge with a hungry look on his face.

"No dinner again tonight then?" He asks flatly, knowing full well that we have been out all day and so the answer is no.

"I haven't prepared anything, if that's what you're asking? But I have entertained three children all day." I say sarcastically and he instantly realises that he should keep his mouth shut if he wants feeding.

"What about jacket potatoes?" I suggest as I take my coat off.

"Look, I'm not being funny but I'm not as 'in' to jacket potatoes as you lot all are!" He says pulling a face before pleading like a small child. "Can we have something else for a change please?" *How about making yourself something then!?* I make a suggestion. "Well, as two out of the three kids had a big lunch and so probably aren't that hungry, shall we take a vote on what to have?"

"Woohoo why not." He replies a little too sarcastically than is polite as he raises an eyebrow.

"Right, the choices are all simple to make because quite frankly I just want to sit down too. So it's either spaghetti bolognaise, omelette or cold meat and mash." I state matter-of-factly and await an argument but I'm wrong.

"Spaghetti!" Dick says so fast and so loud that I nearly jump out of my skin and the boys all nod their heads in agreement.

"Alright grow up" I reprimand him and cast him a silly look, to which he pokes his tongue out in response.

As we eat our dinner, I tell him about my chance meeting again with Annabelle and how the boys all know each other.

"Well I never!" He jokes at my expense. "You never know you may end up being life-long friends?"

13

Less wine, more water!

On Friday morning I run around the house tidying up like a
headless chicken, throwing toys into cupboards and clothes
into the washing machine in preparation for our visitors. I
warn the kids *not* go on about sleepovers while Annabelle
and the boys are here because it's not going to happen as this
is the first time that any of the Bailey family have ever
stepped foot in our house. I'm not convinced they are
listening and they keep accidentally hurting each other with
excitement, so when the door bell rings out at a little after
one o'clock I am relieved to say the least!
As the family enters the three little men are instantly whisked
upstairs, two by two in their 'age pairs' to explore the boys
room, while Annabelle hands me a massive array of cakes
and I can see that there is something for everyone. I point
her in the direction of the kitchen, where I put the kettle on
and we have first pickings on the goodies and when I have
plated up and our cuppa's are ready, we move in to the front
room where I begin to tell her all about my writing,
explaining that this is why I have been into the coffee shop a
few time recently and apologise again for my remark
yesterday. I then move on to describe some of the
characters that I have encountered both in the coffee shop
and elsewhere.
"I was mistaken as a hooker in a Spanish restaurant." I start
and run through the story, now with amusement that
couldn't be shown at the time and go on to tell her about Mr
Smelly too as she listens with obvious amusement.

"Who are your 'victims' from the coffee shop?" She asks inquizically.

"Well... my first pair, after the shitty stains incident, were the two old ladies 'Maud and Madge'. One doesn't shut up and the other can't get a word in". I say and then realise that I should explain myself. "That's obviously my names for them.. or the 'M&M's. The bossy one is..."

"Oh, oh I think I know them! They drag a granny trolley around with them everywhere they go don't they" She shrills excitedly, clapping her hands. *She's getting into it too now!*

"Oh my god, yes that's them!" I shrill back just as excited as she is.

"I bet you wouldn't have guessed that the quiet one is actually a shop lifter would you?!" She continues wide eyed.

"Oh my god, no way!" I say no falling silent, shocked by what I'm being told.

"Yup!" She states, her huge smile tells me that she's pleased with the information she has provided me with.

"Cass, the other girl from the coffee shop." She informs me so that I can keep up with who's who. "Has seen her with her own eyes!" The bossy one walks around nagging and moaning, whilst she walks behind, secretly slipping things into the granny trolley."

"Well bugger me, I am shocked! I always felt a bit sorry for her, I don't any more... thieving cow!" I say, slightly put out by how wrong my instincts were about her.

"Yup I was too! They say that you should watch out for the quiet ones don't they, well it's definitely true in this case." She giggles.

"Yeah." I agree before continuing onto the next case study. "Oh then there was the business man 'Mr O'. Who sat in the corner hiding behind his laptop screen. He got his rocks off by perving over 'Ms Slutty'." I say over excited.

"Mr O... Ms Slutty?" She says confused.

"Oh yeah sorry! Mr Ordinary and Ms Slutty." I update her, before quickly picking up where I left off. "I have never seen anyone drink a drink more seductively in my life! 'Mr. O' looked like he would explode with excitement watching her."

"Oh my god, I know them too!" She squeals excitedly, nearly wetting herself laughing. "Now she really *is* a hooker!"

"No really, she is!" She repeats and I am truly shocked. "Nooooo...!!!!!" I shout back at her, placing a hand over my now open mouth.

"Oh yeah! They have this routine... " She pauses to add to the drama of her story. "He waits in the same spot once a fortnight and she comes in and..." She pauses again before roaring with laughter. "Well you've witnessed yourself what she does! Her little 'show'. We always put the Diet Coke music on when she comes in and watch from out the back, it's just wrong isn't it!"

"Bloody pervert, I knew it!!! Do'ya know what I actually clocked the music too, how funny is that!" I say, trying to look disgusted through my laughter.

"His wife and daughter would not be happy!"

"What?" Annabelle stops dead, looking slightly perturbed.

"What?" I look back at her confused and then realise that she's wondering why on earth I know so much about this man's life. "Oh, I saw him with his family in the food court area last week and I can assure you that he was nowhere near as interested in them as he was Ms Slutty!"

"You really are a stalker!" Annabelle jokes and we both laugh so hard that we have to cross our legs.

"You're right, that does sound stalkerish." I admit before defending myself. "But it's totally innocent, really it is! What happened was, I went past the coffee shop and saw that you were working and after the 'spillage' incident decided to give the place a bit of a long reign. So I changed my 'spying' position to the main eating area and he was there, reading his paper and totally ignoring his family!"

Hopefully this explanation will justify why I was avoiding her.
"Sleazy bastard!"   She agrees nodding her head and I hope that that has excused my silly remark.
"Lucky the page three girls have all gone from the newspapers or you just know what he would have been ogling at!"   She says whilst cupping her hands and pretending that she has massive boobs.
"Eeerrr gross!"   I laugh.
"I can't believe you were avoiding me!"   She comments, a little hurt.
"I know, who would have thought that you'd be here today!"
"Out of interest, who were you spying on when you had your 'spillage incident' by the way?"   Annabelle enquires jovially and continues smirking.   "Because it looked to me like you were perving yourself young lady!"
"Actually, that was my first attempt at spying."   I admit in a sensible voice but still laughing.   "And I was observing the young couple, that's all."
"It wasn't very discrete was it?!"   She quite rightly points out and then almost spits her tea out as she recalls the memory, before concluding "It was very entertaining though, you had me and Cass in fits all afternoon!"
"Hhhmmm... it wasn't so funny for me I can assure you.   I picked the kids up from school looking like that, I don't think it done their street cred much good.... their Mother collecting them looking as though she'd shit herself!"   I say huffily but still smiling.
"Oh no, how funny!   I'm sure someone would have mentioned it by now if it had of been noticeable."   Annabelle laughs.
We talk for hours, intermittently interrupted by the boys coming down from upstairs to wrestle, tell us stories or with request for food or drinks.   It's only when we hear the key in the door at around five thirty that we realise that we haven't stopped talking all afternoon.

"Woohoo it's the weekend!!!!" Booms Dicks voice, as he pushes the front door open so hard that it bangs against the wall, making us both jump.

"Daddy!!!!" Shout the boys as they run down the stairs to greet him.

"Hi boys." He shouts in a funny voice before turning his attention to the Bailey brothers. "And who are these little monkeys?"

"These are... Charlie" Lloyds says pointing to Charlie.

"Jack." He slides his finger across to Jack.

"And this little dude is Harry." He points before joining Harry and affectionately squeezing him.

"Well hello Charlie, Jack and Harry! Who hasn't had a wrestle today?" He asks them all whilst playfully raising his fists at them.

"Me, Me!!" They all scream back and as Dick enters the front room, all six of them follow and hang off of his arms and legs.

"Right!!!!" He roars and chases them all around the front room before looking up and noticing that Annabelle is in the room.

"Oh hi." He says, now rather embarrassed as he is being pulled about by the group of boys.

"Hi, it's lovely to meet you. I'm Annabelle." She pauses and looks over to me and laughs. "I'm the one that your wife has been trying to avoid for the past few weeks, you've probably heard all about me." *Okay, you've made me suffer enough now!*

"Oh yes, now I know." He laughs and I give them both a dirty look.

"I recognise you but I don't know where from?" She says and looks up at the ceiling as if to recall a situation.

"Erm, maybe from the restaurant last week?" He says and then instantly looks at me to see whether he was right to mentioned it or not and I roll my eyes secretly at him, while he tries to flick the boys off.

"Restaurant?" She questions him.

"See, I am a good spy!" I laugh, trying to make light of it.
"Well, I don't know about that." Dick and Annabelle say at the exact same time, much to both of their amusements and the boys all call out 'jinx'.
"Oh yesssss!!" She belts out, cackling. "Oh my god, that was! That was you two!"
 "Erm." We say, looking at each other slightly puzzled.
"You were SO pissed! We watched you both pretending to hide against the walls outside, with fake guns in your hands, whilst you waited for you cab." She says totally amused.
"Oh yeah... that *was* us." I say totally embarrassed as I recall the scene but in all honesty, I can't really recall a lot about that night.. Wincing as I turn to look at Dick, who's doing the same and probably wishing that he had kept his big mouth shut.
"Do you think that everyone saw?" I ask optimistically.
"Hell yeah!! It was SO funny, the whole restaurant was watching! Reckon you were the talking point for most people's Sunday lunches the next day." She carries on, loving the fact that we can obvious recall very little.
"Oh god really, that bad?" I ask, hiding behind my hands. She scrunches up her nose slightly and looks at both of us individually. "Yeah, sorry! You may want to leave it a while to go back there."
"Right, that's it... I'm not drinking again!" I say firmly.
"Don't worry, you didn't offend anyone, it was hilarious." She reassures me.

Mental note - I know that this is one that features a lot... but to drink less wine!

"Do you want a wine girls?" Dick calls out from the kitchen.
"Yeah, go on then." I say and am instantly cross at myself for my lack of self control.
"That drinking ban didn't last long then." He laughs, his words echoing my own thoughts. "Annabelle?"

"Just a little one please, I have to drive this mob home."
She says, sticking her tongue out at the kids who have now
returned to wrestling each other on the lounge floor.
Dick brings our drinks into us and disappears upstairs. The
boys follow and within minutes the noise levels are double
what they have been all day, so I assume he's tormenting
them again.
"Don't wind them all up!" I shout up to him and roll my
eyes at Annabelle.
"Mike's exactly the same." She assures me. "Then, ten
minutes later he'll want to sit down and will expect them all
to calm down, just like that."
"Yup, same thing happens here." I moan.
"Bloody men!" We say at exactly the same time and have to
laugh.
After another half an hour passes Annabelle attempts to
round up her boys, as they strongly protest.
"Please can they have a sleepover Mum? We'll behave."
John starts with his plea and I give him the 'we've already
spoken about this' face but speak in a totally contrasting
tone. "Not tonight darlin'."
"Oh please!" Lloyd backs him up and I give him the same
expression.
"Oh please!" The Bailey brothers join in.
"No. Maybe another night." I state firmly and hope that
this will be an end to it.
"Can't Annabelle stay for a wine?" John asks and I instantly
realise that most kids would have said 'cup of tea'.
"I've had one sweetie... that's how long we've been here!"
Annabelle tries to help me out with this now awkward
conversation.
"Can't you have another one?" He pleads with her.
"No, I'd be drunk! And then who would take these lot
home? She replies but he's too quick for that.
"No-one! They could stay here! You could too?" He says
hopefully, smiling at her.

"We'll come back another day, or you could come to us. Maybe then you could all have a sleepover." She says diplomatically.

"You're more than welcome to leave your car here and stay for a curry?" I whisper. "Mike could join us too?"

"Oh no really, it's too much. We've been here all day, I bet you can't wait to get shot of us all?" She says, looking at her boys whilst considering my invitation.

"Don't be silly, I've had a lovely afternoon *again* and anyway it would be lovely to put a face to the name, now that I've heard so much about him. " I say, honestly meaning it.

"Okay, I'll call Mike and see what he says." She gives in and picks up her mobile phone from the side in the hall to call him.

They make a plan for her to leave the boys with us, while she collects him and then the pair will return and join us for a curry and after she leaves Dick comments how pretty she is, I dig him in the ribs and as I joke that 'Mike' will be eye candy for me too just the doorbell rings and I cover my mouth with my hand, in an attempt to push the words back in, in case they may have overheard.

"Hey come in." Dick says waving the pair into the lounge as he closes the front door behind them.

"Daddy!" On hearing his voice, the Bailey brothers fly down the stairs, just as mine had an hour or so before to greet him.

"Hey, it's my little men!" He said affectionately, whilst tussling with them and Annabelle rolls her eyes at me.

"God, you've duplicated... there's six of you horrible lot now arrhhh!"

"Don't get them all excited, they've been so good." She warns him.

"Alright Mum!" He says sarcastically, whilst Dick laughs at his humour and I instantly know that the pair will get on.

And they do, just as easily as I had fallen into conversation with Annabelle, Dick and Mike spend the evening talking, laughing and reminiscing about their misspent childhoods. They stay until around midnight, when Annabelle stands up to find that she can't now walk straight and Mike decides that it's time for them all to leave. He calls a cab and when it's arrives their shattered boys are far more willing to give in their fight to stay. We thank them for a lovely evening and after they leave pretty much go straight to bed, slightly squiffy and overly tired.

We're all glad of the late night though when, on Saturday morning the boys allow us a small lie in but the minute I open my eyes, my head is banging! I beg Dick to get me some ibuprofen so that I can at least make an attempt to feel normal before moving out of my pit but he tells me that I have no self control and that I will have to get them myself. But minutes late, with the threat that I wouldn't make anyone any breakfast he soon reappears with a cup of tea and hands two pills as he casts me a silly look. As I move myself into an upright position, the Nurf gun from underneath my pillow falls to the floor.

"Why on earth have you got a pretend gun under your pillow?" He asks shaking his head, obviously thinking that I was planning to shoot him when he came to bed last night, in my drunken haze.

"It was a present from John." I say. I am now slumped against the headboard, eyes closed and not daring to move in case it brings the sick up.

"Really?" He asks, unconvinced. "God I can't believe that everyone could see us outside the restaurant."

"Yes really. Long story. Can't speak. Feel sick." I reply, without opening my eyes.

"I'm not even going to ask." He says putting an end to the conversation as he leaves the room sniggering to himself.

"Right, what are we having for breakfast... gooey eggs maybe or bacon?"

Oh my god, I can feel the sick rise to the back of my throat.
"Go away!" I tell him firmly, still frozen in my position with closed eyes.
"Oh your pathetic!" Boys, your Mother's hung over." He pauses and I already know what the annoying sod is planning. "Go and jump all over her, she'll love it!"
And with that the youngest two are in bed with me. I use my hot cup of tea as an excuse why they can't jump on me and it temporarily works. Lloyd doesn't join us he's way too busy in his own room, I can hear the TV playing away and know by his silence that again he is on the iPad too. *Whoever said that men couldn't multi-task haven't met this rare little creature!*
I put my cup down and the boys instantly try to wrestle me.
"Please leave me alone boys." I beg but it's no use, their Father has just given the go ahead to annoy me and they aren't going to pass this opportunity up for love nor money. And so, after about half an hour, I give in. I muster up the energy to get out of bed and trot downstairs, where my only offering for breakfast is cereal. I do not have the stomach to cook this morning and despite the moans, everyone eats.

Mental note - If I can't stick to drinking less wine, then I should try to remember to drink water in between glasses, this is not good!

Later we all reveal our lottery numbers for this week's draw. Mine are: '1' The amount of days of peace I have had this week. '10' The amount of days the boys will have had off of school and '3' woohoo three days until they go back to school... I follow this up with some whooping and am set upon by them all, for being mean.
Dick chooses: '5' The amount of times that he has had to make his own packed lunch this week *(this subsequently ends up with me lecturing him about how lucky he should consider himself during term time, when his beautiful wife makes it for him).* '51' The hours he has worked this week and '59' with absolutely no explanation why... but I'm guessing it's because it's the highest number *again.*

Lloyd picks: '6' The total number of children in our family and the Bailey family combined. '8' The number of whimpy kid diaries he has read now and '48' because four doubled is eight and is an even number. *I'm seriously starting to worry about him?!*

John chooses '6' for the same reason as Lloyd. '32' because that is how many cards he requires to complete his football card collect and '50' Daddy's age and as he says this he makes a run for it because he knows that he's being cheeky and will get wrestled for it.

As standard, I pick '3' for Henry, who is nowhere to be seen this morning and so I figure that must be up to something he shouldn't be. I send Lloyd off to find him and they appear Lloyd is cracked up as he proudly introduces Henry to us, his naked little body is covered from head to toe in his felt tipped 'art work' (if that's what you can call it). *Great!?*

So, with everyone happy and in agreement, this week's lottery numbers are as follows + one lucky dip:

Line One: 1, 3, 10, 48, 51 and 59.

Line Two: 3, 5, 6, 8, 32 and 50.

As usual, we're ready and hyped up for the draw but as usual there's no win for us this week... *boohoo!!*

14

I am really going to miss this lot!

Monday is an inset day and the boys last day off. So I
decide to take them to my favourite place - the seaside! I
invite my Mum and Dad along, I know that this is their
favourite place on earth too. As I pack up the car with
buckets, spades, packed lunches and all sorts of other things
I dust down the seats and shove all of the books, toys and
sweet wrappers into the pockets at the back of the chairs, in
a feeble attempt to tidy the car in preparation for our journey
and avoid Mums telling off. We're half an hour late by the
time that we reach their house but of course, they aren't
ready anyway. I make the boys stay in the car to save time
and go inside to get them up a bit. Dad is just brushing his
teeth and Mum is filling sandwich bags with all sorts of
goodies for the journey from her mini 'shop'.
"Do the boys want crisps?" She asks.
"No, they're alright thanks." I answer and consider it best
not to join her in there otherwise we might not leave for
another half an hour.
"Do they want a sausage roll each? What about you?" She
calls out again from the garage.
"No don't worry about us honestly, I've done us a packed
lunch each but thanks anyway." I call back, hoping that this
will hurry her progress up slightly.

"What about drinks? You have got enough drinks for them haven't you, you don't want them getting dehydrated. I'll put in some Cappysums in." She concludes, speaking quieter to herself now. By this, I know that she means 'Capri Suns', I don't bother picking her up on her mistake and instead just smile to myself and imagine that Dad is doing the same as I hear him entering the kitchen.

"You could stick a few in but only if you've got enough otherwise don't worry, they all have their school water bottles with them, that they can refill if they need to." I say giving in and walk towards the garage just as she rushes past me in the opposite direction.

"I'm nearly ready, I just need a wee. Sorry love." She says and disappears but then reappears a few minutes later still talking "I called Aunty Dor this morning and got chatting. She was telling me that..."

"Tell me in the car, just concentrate on what you're doing will ya." I interrupt her.

"WILF!!" She scalds the dog, who's following her around and nearly tripping her up with every step she takes.

"WILF... BUGGER OFF!" She shouts again, so loud that it would scare the living daylights out of most people but it's such common practice in this house that no-one even flinches... not even the dog.

"Right, I'm ready." She says and I look at the pile of bags in the hallway that I've got to somehow fit into the car and I wonder what's in them all. I ask in disbelief. "What the hell have you got in those?"

"Oh don't start! Just help me out to the car with them will you." She says, half cross and half joking.

"Jesus!" I laugh as I open the boot and show the kids.

"Boys what room have you got on your laps or on your heads? Look at the gear Nanna's got."

"She's got more than us and there's only her and Grandad!" Observes John with surprise.

"Oh come on, there's plenty of space stop going on the pair of you!" She says, as she gets in the car leaving me to pack the boot and Dad to lock the front door.

"Here, I've brought you a scratch card." She says, handing it to me as I get into the car.

"Oh thanks!" I say, kissing it as I fasten my seat belt.

"I know what a lucky cow you are, I'm not sure that I should give it to you. Actually lets swap." She says, almost pulling it back out of my hands again.

"Oi!" I laugh and a snatch it back. "You can't swap now, you've made your decision and what if you swapped and I won... you'd be gutted!"

I watch her face change as she agrees with me before I begin to scratch away at the card and from the back the boys moan that they don't have one. Mum does the same and is absolutely gutted to find that she has won nothing. I, on the other hand, have won £50, something that I take great pleasure in telling her as I wave the scratch card around in the air.

"You could fall into a bucket of shit and come out smelling of roses!" She complains, shaking her head in disbelief.

"Oh, how glad am I that you didn't swap now!" I giggle and the boys start talking about what *they* want to buy with the winnings.

"Thanks Mum! Right, I think I'll buy the ice creams with this, what do'ya reckon boys." I say and with this they all squeal and clap their hands.

"Hhhmmm... I can't believe your bloody luck!" She grumbles sulkily, although she is smiling.

The traffic isn't too bad on the motorway and so we make good time but this all changes when we hit the towns. There is basically one way in and one way out to this particular beach and although the council have redesigned the area in recent years, there are still constant queues to get in *and* out.

While we wait, Mum tells me all about what she and Aunty Dor spoke about and I update her on what I've been up to. I go on to tell her all about Annabelle, Mike and their boys. Whilst in the back I can hear the boys trying to wake Dad up by singing loudly.

After about an hour we park up in the usual spot, on a road that over-looks the sea front and as we admire the views and breath in the sea air, I tell the boys *(as I do every time we come)* that this is where I want them to scatter my ashes when I die, so that they can visit the seaside every time and that this will cheer them up. *Much to the upset of Lloyd, who refuses point blank to talk about my eventual passing. This is something that John has picked up on and so often asks me questions about 'when I'm a star in the sky', just to upset and wind Lloyd up.*

If I come here with Mercy or Patsy and the girls we usually walk through the alley and down the seventy something steps to get to the bottom of the chalk cliffs, as we did when we were kids. We then usually sit close to where our Grandparents beach hut used to be, where we would go crabbing while we reminisce about our childhood. But these days that's just too many steps for the oldies to battle now and so we park the other end where there is a steep slope instead and walk down to the more popular beach on the corner. *I must say that watching them attempt this slope, scares the bloody life out of me every time!*

We sit on the wall at the entrance to the beach and dangle our feet over the edge, whilst the boys dig out sand to form a boat shape. *Oh I love this place!*

"Shall we get some chips?" Mum asks, looking in the direction of the shops.

"You've got ten thousand bags of food here?" Dad points out, looking down at the copious amounts of luggage we have at our feet with a raised eyebrow. "Didn't you make sandwiches?"

"Yes I did but I can smell them now." She says smiling and sniffing in the air. *Ah 'see it buy it' disease again!*

"I know, why don't we have our packed lunches in a while and then stop in at that nice fish and chips place on our way home?" I suggest, both to keep the peace and for selfish reason, I prefer their chips.

"Good idea." They both agree.

"Shall we have an ice cream instead then?" She suggests after a few minutes of contemplating it.

"Yeah why not, I'll get them.... with my winnings! I gloat with a massive smile on my face as I do a little dance.

"I still can't believe that... ya lucky bitch!" She says, raising an eyebrow and shaking her head once more.

"Ha, ha! Who's coming with me?" I ask, looking around at the boys already knowing that they will all want to come, which is good as I could use their hands.

"Me, Me!" They all shout excitedly as expected and spring to their feet, patting off some of the sand that completely covers their little body's.

We bring back the ice creams but as usual none of the boys finish them because the sand particles are crunching between their teeth and ruining the texture. The seagulls are being a nuisance too, freaking them all out by swooping down and getting dangerously close to pinching them out of their hands. As I laugh at them running around, throwing their little hands up in the air to warn them off, I am reminded of the time that Mercy was eating a crayfish sandwich, whilst sitting alone on a busy beach, waiting for a friend to arrive. As she read her book and unwrapped her sandwich with her free hand, a cheeky seagull swooped down and stole the entire sandwich, leaving her stunned for a few minutes before looking up to see that everyone around her laugh their heads off. So she sat alone, feeling totally embarrassed.

Mental note - To wind her up by telling her that I have actually seen her a clip on YouTube.

The boys and I go for a paddle in the sea and as we return we see a little man walking around ringing a school bell. His clothes are worn out and faded and he has a pretend monkey hanging around his shoulders, cuddling him. The boys instantly know why he's shouting.

"!it's 'Punch and Judy' time! Can we go and watch it?" Cries John.

I nod and watch their little faces beam, as I rummage through my bag to find my purse. I hand them some money and then follow behind as they run along the sand towards the familiar booth. The sand is boiling beneath our feet and so the boys sensibly seat themselves in the shade of the wind breakers, huddled together for comfort. They laugh at 'Punch' as he floors everyone that he comes into contact with, saying 'that's the way to do it', while the kids all shout out 'he's behind you' when prompted, while I note to myself just how politically incorrect every aspect of this show is (but secretly enjoy every minute of this dying seaside tradition).

When it's finished Henry is so pumped up by what he has seen, that he tries to sneak around the back of the booth for a play with the puppets. I spot him just in time and call out, pointing at the puppeteer while warning him that he will be cross if he sees. We slowly make our way back across the beach to rejoin Mum and Dad, where they are sitting back, enjoying the sunshine. We chat about how lovely the day has been and how well behaved the boys have been, when all of a sudden out of the corner of my eye I spot John chalking on the side of one of the beach huts. I stand up and call out to reprimand him but just as I do so, I hear a man yelling from behind me and turn to see what's on earth is happening... and it turns out that he's shouting at me?!

"Oi, your kid's just drawn on my hut!" He shouts out, furiously pointing in the direction of John. But his angry reaction instantly makes me mad too... at him! *Can he not see that I am already sorting it?!*

"I'm sorry, are you talking to me?!" I yell back at him, looking around to check that I haven't misread the scene. "Yeah I am!" He continues his rant, all the while wagging his finger at John who's lip is quivering, as half of the beach turns to stare at us all. "Have you seen what your kid has just done?!"

"Yes I have and can you see what I'm doing?" I pause, throwing my hands up in the air. "I'm telling him off that's what. Well I was before you started shouting your bloody mouth off, interrupting me!"

"Little bastard." He starts again and I almost explode back at him.

"It's chalk you dickhead! It'll rub off! Get a life and stop shouting at little children! This is a beach, a place for *fun*, you horrible *old* man!" I holler, emphasising the 'old' and the 'fun' and I feel as though my face is on fire as I do so. As I come up for breathe, I daren't look at my Mum. She is probably now panicking and imagining *all* sorts of scenarios! After a few more minutes of mumbling to himself, the man walks off and as he disappears John hurries back over to us and cuddles into me like a scared puppy, obviously shaken by what has just happened while Mum and the boys talk at speed about what a wretched old man he was and how they weren't expecting me to react that the way I did. As I calm down, we end up laughing about the fact that a day out with us is never dull and out of principle I don't make John rub the chalk off of this hut, as was going to be his punishment because I think he's suffered enough. *The miserable old bastard can do that himself!*

I suggest that we eat, to give the people on the beach a chance to get back to what they're doing, instead of watching us. But again the bloody seagulls reappear, ruining our lunch and resulting in the boys irritating everyone around us by throwing their sandwiches into the air for the birds to catch and so again we are the centre of attention and not in a good way. *Time to leave me thinks, before they get me into another row!*

We take a short walk around the town and as usual, end up in the arcades. The boys huddle around me, looking not that dissimilar to the seagulls now with their arms stretched out, hands open, pleading for money. I give each of them a few pounds and tell them that under NO circumstances are they allowed to leave the arcade, otherwise we won't be able to find them EVER again *(followed by a lecture on 'stranger danger')*. I then really upset Henry by telling him that he has to stay with me because he's too little to be unsupervised in public places.

Every time we come to the penny machines Mum turns into more of a kid than the kids themselves. She *only ever* plays on the two penny machines, nothing else and once she's on a machine there's no budging her until she has won every prize it contains, which is usually a load of old toot. It's as though she has become obsessed. She bribes the boys with more money, if they go and change her up another pounds worth of two pence coins and she's fixed in her position until we have to literally pull her away. My Dad on the other hand, gets absolutely no joy from the arcades and can usually be found following the boys around, watching them enjoying themselves or outside on a bench eating ice-cream. After about an hour, I suggest leaving and after some initial resistance Mum gives in and once she's out of the 'zone', we all joke about how much money she has spent on items that probably only amount to less than a pound to actually buy from a shop.

We walk back up the hill and pass the hotel that was once the building where Charles Dickens used to stay. We recently paid for Mum and Dad to stay there for a present and during their two night visit, they got friendly with the owners and so pop in to say 'hello' before returning to the car.

"Ah what a lovely day it's been today. I love this place. You can't beat a trip to the seaside!." Says Lloyd from the back seat and for a moment I question whether it was him or Dad that spoke because it was such an adult comment.

"Do you darlin?" I reply, smiling at him in the rear view mirror, hoping that he and the others will bring their children here too and remember days like today.

"Yeah. Can we come back again soon?" He asks looking back at me with tired eyes but I already know that the car journey won't knock him out because this is another one of his weird little ways. Unlike the other two who can fall asleep before the engine has even started, Lloyd has voweled *never* to give in to falling asleep on a car journey... *god only knows what goes on inside that little head of his?*

"Of course we can. You know this is my favourite place in the world!" I assure him.

"Good." Everyone agrees wearily. *I am really going to miss this lot when they go back to school!*

We stop off at the edge of the town, at a little fish and chip shop for our tea and although we have only been in the car for ten minutes, I have to wake both John and Henry up. We sit in to eat and when we have finished, I gather up all of the leftover food into a plastic take away container.

"What's that for?" Mum asks, looking confused.

"Dick's dinner." I tell her.

"Oh Eva" She says in a pitiful voice, looking at all of the half eaten food, piled high. "Don't be mean, get him something too, the poor sod. He's been working all day."

"Nah I've told him to get his own dinner, he'll have had it already. This'll be a little added extra treat for him, to let him know that we haven't forgotten him today on our day out." I say, with a wicked smile on my face, knowing that he actually will love it.

"Nice. Everyone's leftovers." She states in a sarcastic tone. "I would think he'd prefer to be forgotten about, that have to eat that lot." She continues, staring down again at the plastic box that now contains chips, a bit of salami sausage, half a burger and some fish.

"He'll love it! Won't he?" I say and the boys nod in agreement.

"Hhhmmm I'm not so sure."   She says doubtfully and then turns to Dad.   "See, you should count yourself lucky - you could have married someone like her!"

"She perfect, Dick's a lucky man!"   He answers, smiling at me and I smile back, whilst Mum rolls her eyes at us both. She has always joked that I love him a little bit more than her and that he loves all of us girls more than he loves her.

We drop the pair of them off and when we get home the boys lovingly present Dick with the plastic food box and as predicted he is pleased as punch.   *Mainly because he has totally forgotten that I'd told him to sort his own dinner out and is absolutely starving and ready to eat anything he can, as quickly as he can.*   He warms it up and sits down at the table and is instantly joined by Henry, who after an hour's journey is ready for his second helping of food but Dick doesn't like to share and so only lets him have a few chips before sending him upstairs to me, where I am busy bathing the others, ready for school the following morning.   I then lay out all of their uniforms and dutifully go downstairs to prepare the dreaded packed lunches, grumbling inside my head that I can avoid this task for an extra day but when I open the fridge, Dick has made both his and the boys and I am very pleasantly surprised!

Ah ha... see what some leftovers can lead to Mum!

Mental note - To leave making packed lunches to the very last minute in future - that way this may happen more often?!

When they are all in bed, I pour us both a big glass of wine and slouch back on the sofa, feeling totally shattered.   I tell Dick all about 'Old Mr Moany' and the annoying seagulls, while he conveys his inability to believe how my trips out *always* result in drama and sets me a challenge to try to go a full week without any little 'incidents'.   *Easy....!*

15

How do I get myself into these situations?!

On the way back from the school run, I nip to the shops to restock the empty fridge and cupboards in an attempt to prevent arguments later on, when the boys get home from school tired and hungry.   At the counter as I pull my purse out of my a pocket to pay the cashier, a little scrap of yellow paper falls out. I bend down, pick it up and slip it back into my jacket, fastening the zip for safe keeping, as I smile to myself.

Back at the car after packing the shopping into the boot, I sit in the driver's seat and fish around in my pocket to retrieve it once again.   Once found, I hold it in my hands and study it - it's a print out that I was awarded yesterday, from the 'Zoltar Speaks' machine in the arcades.   On one side it has a picture of 'Zoltar' himself, surrounded by star signs and symbols. On the other, it states 'Your fortune'. Zoltar is supposed to be a gypsy fortune teller from the East, like in the film 'Big', where Tom Hanks asks Zoltar to make him big and he grants his wish.

My fortune states:

'I see a great deal of happiness in store for you.   Thousands of candles can be lighted from a single candle and the life of the candle will not be shortened.   Happiness never deceased by being shared.   So, if an object you ardently pursue brings little happiness when gained, remember most of our pleasures come from unexpected sources.   Share the good news when it arrives.
For happiness is like a sunbeam which the least shadow will intercept, while suffering is often as the rain of spring.   Enjoy every day.
Your lucky numbers are: 24,39,21,12,31,04'.

All the way home, I in my mind the meaning of what I have just read.   I convince myself that it's telling me to put all of the horrible people from my the past behind me, to stop trying to find a reason to excuse their behaviours and instead move onwards and upwards and stay happy as it's contagious and makes other people happy too!   *I know this anyway - my mantra in life is to stay positive, to only surround myself with positive people and to remember that you get what you wish for.*
I also feel butterflies in my tummy, as I see this as a great omen for this week's lottery.   *Zoltar's even picked my number choices, so we're sure to win!* With this in mind and full of excitement about Saturdays draw, I begin to imagine my *big win.   Wouldn't you?!* 'See it and it will come', I tell myself as I picture the cheque being presented to us and how happy we all look.   I imagine choosing our new car... no cars, which have TV's in the head rests for the boys to watch. Next up we're looking through holiday brochures, choosing where our next adventure will take place.   I see Dick looking through extension plans and me through garden designs.. and for the entire journey home I'm completely absorbed in my very own fantasy world!
But back in the real world, at home, with the boys at school the house is oddly quiet.   I don't like it, I miss them.   I load the dishwasher and washing machine, to try to make a dent the mess that remains after their week off.

I then turn on the radio for some company and straight away the young male presenter announces a competition that the station is running, for one lucky listener to win £10k by simply texting a word in within an allocated time slot. I instantly pick up my mobile phone and text in again and again until I reach the maximum amount of entries. Taking the coincidence of having turned on the radio at that exact time as a sign that I am destined to win this prize. *One of these days I just know that it'll happen!*

I then fire up my laptop and check out the radio stations website for some more competitions to enter, before making the fatal mistake of signing in to my lottery account. Ten minutes later and ten pounds lighter, I disappointedly sign out and decide that it's time to get on with some work! But it's no use, I just can't focus and so instead I open my novel and start tapping away at the keypad.

It's not until the doorbell rings that I notice it is two thirty already. *God where does the time go when I'm writing?!* I open the front door and there's a brightly dressed lady standing opposite me, she's foreign looking but I can't figure out of which nationality and as I look at her, I wonder whether she got dressed in the dark this morning. *I mean, I'm no fashion guru but even I can see that none of her clothes really go together.*

"Hi, can I help you." I say, trying to decide what on earth she could be selling, looking like that. She then holds up a handmade hand written laminated sign and I instantly feel a pang of guilt for my previous thoughts. It reads..

"Hello, my name Sian I am def and dum. I love to paint. I must sell my art to pay my operashan. Please by £10."

She then pulls out six paintings, all of which are as equally crap as the next, to be blatantly honest. I study them for a while, desperately trying to come up with a reason in my head that I can use to tell her why I can't make a purchase. *Come on, come on!!*

"They are really lovely." I lie, moving my lips dramatically so that she can lip read and am pleased with myself as she nods her head, as though she understands me.

"The problem is that I don't think that I have ten pounds here I'm afraid." I continue apologetically.

She then pulls out of her bag another hand written laminated sign, reading 'a small donashan will help'. *Oh good god, how can I say no now? You've got to love a trier!*

I tell her to hold on and go back inside the house, closing the door behind me and feeling rude for doing so but at the same time worried that she may follow me in if I didn't. I rummage around in my purse. Shit only a twenty pound note, I'm not giving her that! I run upstairs and raid Lloyds penny jar, to find that there's only two pounds in ten and twenty pence's. I know that there isn't any other stashes of money anywhere in the house and so this will have to do, even if it looks as though I've scraped the bottom of the barrel.

I silently stand for a while, wondering whether if I don't return she would get the hint and leave. But after a few minutes I feel too guilty and head back downstairs. As I re-open the door and hand over the fistful of coins, I apologetically lie about the shortfall in payment, saying that I'd give her more if I had it whilst trying to push the picture of the twenty pound note into the corner of my mind. But to my utter shock, she has already gathered up the paintings and laminates and just takes the money, without thanks and then turns to leave.

"Erm excuse me!" I call after her, feeling slightly put out but still trying to stay polite. "What about the painting?" She looks at me, looks down at the pile of silver coins in her hand and then looks at me again, as if to say 'you didn't pay me enough', which instantly irritates me. *I could have told her to piss off and given her nothing, rude cow!*

"I gave you money, you gave me nothing?" I say slowly, still emphasising my lips as I speak but feeling less guilty and even more annoyed, as she again looks down at the pile of loose change and then back to me, before shaking her head.

"Right, well I'll have my money back then!" I say pettily, stretching out my arm and opening my palms ready to receive my refund.

With this, she opens her bag again and pulls out a small A5 painting, which is ruffled at the edges like a piece of scruffy homework and I notice that it is a smaller copy of the original crap that she showed me. She places it into my open hands and turns to leave again, whilst I stand watching her from behind in silenced disbelief. I scold myself for being so gullible, as I come to the realisation that she can't be deaf because she had her back towards me when I called out to her. *Thieving witch!*

Mental note - Not to be so easily fooled in future. Just say 'no' and close the door to anyone that knocks on the door uninvited!

I come inside and contemplate binning the painting but instead prop it up on the windowsill in the kitchen, alongside some of the kids drawings and the three seed pots, that came home with the kids from school a few months ago. Two of these plants, whatever they are, have grown totally out of control and the other is half dead but I can't throw any of them away as it will cause arguments and accusations of favouritism - even though I'm the only one that ever waters them and so technically they are all mine) I will show the painting to the kids later on and use it to warn them again about stranger danger... and about being ripped off.

I suddenly realise that this little episode has taken up the remaining time that I had before I needed to leave to collect the boys. I hurry out of the house grabbing my coat, purse and phone as I go and jump into the car. Half way up the road, I spot the devil women again and have to look twice as I notice that she's on the bloody phone. I'm instantly enraged and so pull up on the pavement alongside her and beep my horn as though I'm about to run her over, making her nearly jump out of her skin..

"Oh! You heard that okay didn't you!" I yell as I wind down the passenger window.

She doesn't say anything, just stares at me as though I'm crazy.

"You robbing bitch, there's nothing wrong with you! You should be ashamed of yourself! The poor deaf people of this world would have a thing or two to say about your conduct, I'm sure!""

"Spear-die-lie!" She yells back at me and I can only presume that she has just sworn at me or told me to drop dead by the angry face that accompanies the quote.

"Oh and suddenly you have a voice too!" I rant, still shouting. Then, by sheer coincidence just at that very moment a policeman approaches the car. *Oh god, where did he pop up from... right, count from ten backwards and calm down.*

"Okay, what seems to be the issue here ladies?" He asks, frowning at me as though I'm to blame and I'm quick to defend myself.

"This women knocked on my door less than ten minutes ago, pretending to be deaf and dumb and flogging crap paintings to raise money for an operation! And look at her, there's nothing wrong with her.

"Is this true?" He questions the women.

"I speak little English." She says shrugging her shoulders and shaking her head, as if she has no idea what he is asking or why I'm attacking her. As she says this holds out her thumb and forefinger to form the international sign for 'small'.

"You speak though don't you. You're definitely not dumb!" I say and then pause as I realise that I still sound aggressive before adding. "Well not in that sense anyway!"

"Okay madam." The policeman says, trying to silence me.

"Were you or were you not, knocking on peoples doors asking for money?" He asks her slowly, using the same lip gestures that I had done previously and with that she tries to make a run for it but he's too fast, he catches and handcuffs her after just a few paces and then radios in to the station for a car to come and collect them both. *Ah ha, have that!*

"Did you give her any money?" He asks and I feel extremely embarrassed now, not so much because I was foolish enough to have given her money but more because now I have to admit how much and all of a sudden this all seems a bit petty.

"Yes I did officer." I state, trying to dodge the inevitable question.

"Can I ask how much?" He prods.

"Well, she wanted ten pounds but I only had two and so gave her that." I say and quickly add. "But it's not about the money that I'm cross about, it's the fact that she conned me. She could and maybe has taken a lot more from a vulnerable or an old person." I say caringly. *Although I have to be honest, this hadn't actually crossed my mind before now.*

"You stand there and don't move." He tells her, steering the women in the direction of my car bonnet.

"Look in her bag, you'll see the shit paintings that she's showing people!" I instruct him, pointing my finger out of my window at her bag.

"We'll take a look down the station, when my college arrives." He says with authority and I take the hint to shut up.

"So, I'm going to have to take your name and address please." He continues.

Oh shit!

"This is a very serious accusation that you have made about this women, you'll need to come down to the station to make a statement and if she is found guilty and it goes to court, we will need to contact you again." He informs me.

How do I get myself into these situations? What will Dick say?
He'll probably gloat about how I haven't even made it through day one
of his challenge before messing up. Oh god and court too?!

Mental note - To not enter into challenges that are quite frankly going
to be impossible to achieve!

"Oh bollocks!" I blurt out loudly without thinking, as I look
over at the dashboard and notice the time. With this, he
stops speaking momentarily into his walky-talky and looks
over at me with surprise.
"Sorry." I apologise before explaining in more detail. "I've
just noticed the time, I'm late collecting my children from
school."
"Well if you wouldn't mind, before you go." He asks again
politely.
"No worries and then I really have to go." I say, whilst
scribbling my name and address onto the back of one Johns
drawings that I have found lying on the passenger seat.
As I hand him my details, I catch a glimpse of the other side
of the drawing and realise instantly that I should take it back
but it's too late, he already has it in his grasp. The drawing
is of a naked man who's willy comes down to his knees, he
has messy hair and a glass of wine in his hand. Written next
to him is the word 'Moobs' and there's a arrow pointing at
his nipples. *Good god, what will they make of that back at the*
station?!
"And if you could come down to the station sometime this
evening please, that would be helpful too." He requests,
putting the paper into his pocket as he nods to signify that it
is okay for me to leave. *Please let him lose that along the way!*
I nod back at him and am off again, calling the school as I go
to explain why I am late *(using a complete lie as an excuse rather*
than the actual truth... I don't want them thinking I'm a complete
nutter).

I go straight to the office and find the three of them sitting in the comfy chairs, reading books in the reception waiting area and as they see me approach, their little faces tell me all I need to know... they are cross!

"I'm really sorry guys!" I say quickly as I enter and then apologise to the receptionist too, who smiles and shakes her head, to signal that it's not a problem.

"Where were you? I was scared that something had happened to you!" John says, obviously upset which makes me feel really bad too.

"Oh darlin', I am sorry! I got held up by a *silly* lady." I begin to explain, emphasizing the word silly and then wishing that I could pop the words back into my mouth as I realise that this is not the story that I have just told the receptionist. I quickly glance over to her but luckily, she is too busy typing away at her computer to hear my slip up.

Mental note - To remember my lies!

"I'll explain on the way." I tell him, ushering them all out of the double doors and over to the car park, where unbeknownst to me when I pulled up, my car is illegally parked in a disabled space. *I NEVER do this, in fact I usually moan about people that do and so instantly feel terrible. I scold myself as we walk towards it but then quickly stop before the boys pick up on what I've done too!*

"I'm hungry." Complains John.

"Okay, well we kind of need to go to the police station now. But I've been shopping and so will stop off at home on the way and grab you a snack first." I pacify him.

"Oh wow... the police station!" He yells and I look in my rear view mirror to see that his eyes lit up.

"I've always wanted to see inside a police station!" He continues excitedly. *Let's hope you calm down a bit before you're eighteen, otherwise you may see it more than you should!*

"Are you in trouble Mummy?" Enquires Lloyd as he spins his face around to look at me with obvious concern. I smile at him to make him feel better and it works, he relaxes and smiles back at me.

"No, not me. I had a bit of a run in with a bad lady today..." I start and then tell them all about it. *(Followed by the lecture that I had planned for later, about stranger danger and fraudsters as it felt like the right time).* We park up outside the station and John is the first to jump out of the car, hopping from foot to foot, trying to hurry me up.

"Mummy's only got to write some things down and then we're going home. We're not going to see the cells or anything " I say, trying to calm him.

"Aaaww." He moans.

"I've looked around before, with Cubs." Lloyd gloats and again he has got 'one up' on the others but they just ignore him anyway.

We enter the station and I explain why we are here. A few moments later, a police officer comes out from behind the locked doors and asks the boys whether they would like to have a look around, while I make my statement. John gasps and looks over at me and I think that he is about to explode.

"Oh yes please!" He says in a high pitched tone and the biggest smile on his face.

"Is that okay with you Mum?" The officer asks kindly.

"Yes it's fine, if you don't mind." I say and hope that none of them say anything inappropriate while they are in his company. *I would usually give them 'the talk' about being sensible, before something like this.*

"Behave yourselves boys please, no running off and listen to the officer!" I warn them and they know that the look I am giving them, says that 'I mean what I say', so that they know there will be consequences should they misbehave.

"I'm sure they'll be fine. If not I'll throw them in a cell!" He jests and with that John jumps with joy and bends down to show his excitement to Henry, who squeals too, although not actually knowing why.

"I'll go with them Mum. To look after them because I have seen this all before." Lloyd explains, so that I know that it's definitely not for his benefit (yeah right). I have a feeling that he is going to boss them about in my absence.

"Thanks darlin'." I say and begin writing my statement.

It only takes about ten minutes and as I sit and wait for the boys to return, I can hear them before I see them and can tell that they have enjoyed their visit. I thank the officer and we all say our goodbyes and just before we leave the officer that was at the scene appears and hands me back the drawing with my details on from earlier, joking that whoever is in the picture may be proud to see it *(obviously meaning the size of his willy)*.

"I think it's supposed to be his Dad." I say jokily and then wonder whether that just sounded wrong *(but surely better than if he had drawn anyone else's willy)*.

"Hey that's mine!" John says, pulling it out of my hands and laughing.

"Goodbye." I say.

"Look at Daddy's peanuts." He giggles as he points it out while I smile, red faced and make for the doors just as my phone rings, which I ignore. I can imagine that our ears will be burning later.

"We're not parked in a disabled spot again are we?" Asks Lloyd and I give him a dirty look. "What?! You did earlier! Mrs Warden told us all in assembly the other day that..."

"That was a mistake, I didn't realise it was a disabled spot." I interrupt him, mortified again to recall this and literally push him out of the doors to shut him up and into the fresh air, which my cheeks now really appreciate!

Mental Note - To be more careful what I say around little ears!!

Back in the car my mobile rings again, just as the phone connects to the car speakers.

"Where are you all?" Asks Dick. He has probably been home for the last hour, enjoying the peace and quiet but is only now wondering where we are because he is getting hungry, not because he is concerned.

"I'll explain when I get..." I say feeling harassed.
"We've been to have a look around the police cells!" John
pipes up, still over excited from the back seat.
"Oh god, what have you got yourself into now Eva?" He
asks, sighing in disbelief as though he's speaking to a child.
"Nothing! We'll be home in ten minutes, I'll tell you then.
Oh sorry I can't hear you very well" I say and promptly
hang up, pretending that I'm having difficulty with the signal.
At home I update him on what has happened, show
everyone the painting that accompanied my earlier lecture
and as expected, Dick gets all high and mighty about always
being right and I sulkily agree that in this instance *(and only
this one),* he is right and has won the challenge.

16

A bad influence!

After the trauma of Tuesday, I have decided that I need some time at home. Time to catch up on the washing, housework and all of the other crap jobs that I've been putting off and to my surprise, it's not until Thursday afternoon that I finally get straight again. At around two o'clock Hazel, a friend calls to ask whether I could pick up her son from school because she's stuck in traffic and not going to make it back in time. She tells me not to worry about her daughter, she's going back to a friend's house and so will be fine. Her son Tom is in a different year to mine and so I decide to pick him up first, suspecting that he would enjoy greeting the others at their classrooms with me and breaking the exciting news that he is coming home to play. As I stand outside his classroom I spot a Mum that I'd been avoiding, following a misunderstanding that ended up badly *(not my fault, I would like to add)*. I turn away from her to save any awkwardness and spot Roxy walking towards me.
"Hi. What are you doing over here?" She asks me, with a look that says 'are you loosing the plot'.
"I'm picking up Hazels 'Tom'." I explain.
She then lowers her tone and of course I know why. "Have you seen who's behind you?" She says lifting her eye's in the direction of 'the enemy' and laughs. *"Awkward!"*
"I know!" I say quietly, without allowing my eyes to follow her gaze.

"Psycho bitch!" She says wickedly, openly staring at the recipient whilst screwing her nose up.

"Look at her scrawny little body... eerrhh." This comment really makes me laugh not only because the women is painfully skinny but more because I love her unconditional loyalty towards me.

"Do you want me to wait with you?" She asks protectively.

"No, you're alright mate! You'll be late to collect yours otherwise." I assure her.

"Sure?" She checks.

"Sure!" I say, with a thankful smile. *I love my friends!*

"Sure you're sure?" She checks again smiling.

"Absolutely, sure I'm sure, I'm sure." I say and we both laugh, before cuddling and she heads off.

Tom comes out and I can see the excitement fill his little eyes, as he realises that he will be coming home with us for a play date. He's a sweet looking little thing and a typical 'boy'. He gets on with all of my kids but particularly likes Lloyd because he's older. Lloyd is very fond of him too, he can sense Toms ore and takes full advantage of this power by showing off all of the interesting facts that he knows.

"Shall we go and get the boys?" I ask him, taking his bag and slinging it over my shoulder. Just as I do so, I feel the bag hit the person behind, somewhere in their facial region. As I turn, apologising, I instantly cut my sentence short as I realise that it's 'the enemy' that I have just clobbered and instead end by giving her an evil look and as I walk away I hear her muttering something about me but don't grace her with retaliation. *Remember.. no dramas for the rest of the week, at least!!*

At home Hazel arrives just after five with her daughter April and her husband Fred, a friend of Dicks, just as I'm dishing up the dinner. I manage to stretch it out between us all, while she thanks me for being a life saver and passes me a bottle of wine.

"Well, it's rude not to isn't then?!" I say, waving the bottle at her. "Who's driving?"

"Fred can after the day I've had. I'll join you with a wine please." She says with no consultation and I spot Fred raising an eyebrow. I open the bottle, pour two large glasses and hand one to her. She takes a massive gulp as if to say 'I need this', that surprises me and we both giggle.

After dinner the men sit at the table in the dining room discussing work, the kids disappear upstairs and we retreat to the front room. The usual topics are covered and the wine flows. And as the time goes by, I gradually put all three of my kids to bed, to avoid morning arguments because they are over tired and a little after nine thirty Hazel notices their absence.

"Where 'ave ya kids gone?" She asks, slightly slurring.

"In bed, otherwise tomorrow morning would just be a nightmare." I explain, feeling a bit mean.

"What's the time then?" She asks, looking confused.

"It's nearly ten o'clock." I laugh as she's fumbling to check her watch.

"Do you feel pissed?" I ask laughing.

"I didn't... but all of the sudden I do!" She giggles and then yells out, making me jump. "FRED!"

But there's no response from the dining room, the two men are in deep conversation.

"FRED!" She calls again even more loudly that I think even over the road heard.

"FRED! We're going home! Do'ya know what time it is?! The kids 'ave got school in the morning!" She shouts again, slurring her words even more now before getting up in an attempt to hurry him along but as she does, she falls back down again, looking around at me and giggling even more.

"Jesus, how 'd I get so drunk? It's your bloody fault!" She says, blaming me as we laugh and laugh as the men come into the front room to see what's going on.

"You're not even ready, why are you shouting at me?" Asks Fred, looking slightly disgusted at the state she's in.

"Coz we've gotta go!" She says closing her eyes and lying backwards on the sofa.

"Bloody hell, how drunk are you?" He asks noticeably shocked at the change in her from an hour ago, when he had come in to see when she wanted to leave because he wanted to go to bed at a reasonable time.

"It's 'er fault!" She says, wagging her finger at me. Again she attempts to stand up and this time actually managing it.

"Hhhmm... Eva doesn't look like you do!" He says smiling at Dick and me before walking over to her, picking her up and throwing her over his shoulder.

"Jesus don't do that, I think I'm going to throw up!" She laughs.

"I'd better get her home." He tells Dick and then warns Hazel not to throw up in the car otherwise she'll be cleaning it not him.

"Come on kids, ya Mothers drunk!" He says as we all say our goodbyes and as they leave Hazel tries to bear hug her children but they push her away while rolling their eyes at us in mock embarrassment. We wave them off from the door step and as we lie in bed laugh at how bad she will feel in the morning.

And as expected when I spot Hazel on the school run, walking towards me as I'm on my way back to the car she looks terrible.

"Running a bit late are you?" I ask brightly, laughing. "How you feeling?"

"Oh my god, rough!" She says dryly.

"Look, I've even done a 'you'." She says and I giggle as she pulls a carrier bag out of her pocket. *This is my little trick, to try to make hangovers a bit more bearable I take a sick bag out with me.. just in case!*

"Oh dear! It was a lovely evening though wasn't it!" I say, smiling. *God I'm glad it's her and not me feeling like that!*

"Yeah it was.. from what I remember? Thanks again, ya bitch!" She laughs as she pulls her sleeve back and checks her watch. "Oh shit, we'd better go, we are *so* late!"

"See you later, I hope you feel better soon!" I call after her.

"Yeah, cheers!" She says, looking exhausted and scurrying off, dragging the kids behind her, as their little legs go ten to the dozen.

Mental note - To always try to be this responsible because it feels gooood not to be the most hung-over person!

On my walk back to the car I call Mercy.

"Hiya, you okay?" I ask as she answers the phone.

"Yeah, good cheers. You?" She asks.

"I'm good. Dicks working tomorrow, so we're coming over." I inform her without asking.

"Oh right, are you now?!" She laughs but I know she's pleased.

"Yup. Let me know when you're up and about and whether you want us to bring anything and we'll be there." I instruct her before hanging up.

And as promised, Saturday lunchtime we descend on mass at Mercy's house but she's prepared, she has brought in all of the things that she knows everyone likes and for the first half an hour all you can hear is 'Aunty M can I have this... Aunty M can I do this...' and she lovingly deals with each request, like a good Aunty should. We have a lovely day spent out in the garden, she lets the boys chalk all over her stone stabs and we play 'it' until I laugh so much after nearly knocking Mercy out whilst 'it-ing' her that I actually wet myself *(much to the kids disgust)!* And when it's time to leave, the boys protest so much that she gives in and lets them stay the night. On hearing the news, I practically run out of the house before she can change her mind and call Dick enroute home to tell him to get his glad rags on because we've got an unexpected date night.

We walk down to the local pub and order a pint each, feeling extremely pleased with the temporary freedom that we have been awarded and later that night go for a sit down curry, to avoid the temptation of being delivered home again and eat it without having to share. *Oh this is the life! The boys would be jealous!*

17

To tell or not to tell?

Early Sunday morning the phone rings out. *What the hell?!*
I open my eyes and jump out of bed, worried that it could be
Mercy telling me that something's happened with one of the
boys. But instead it's Mum.
"Hi." She says.
"Jesus! Have you shit the bed?" Is my initial response
when I find out that it's her and then realise that what I have
said is a rather inappropriate thing to say to a parent.
"No, we're going out today aren't we?!" She states, as
though I should know this.
"Oh are we?" I say sleepily, climbing back into my bed,
wishing that I hadn't answered the phone.
"You know we are!" She responds huffily, mythed that I
haven't remembered.
"Oh yeah, sorry." I say, closing my eyes and wondering
whether I can get away with just yes/no answers and go back
to sleep.
"Oh, don't tell me you've forgotten?" She questions me.
"No." I say, drifting back off to sleep.
"Why aren't you here then?" She asks.
"Yes." I answer, realising that if 'no' wasn't the right answer
then 'yes' must be.
"EVA!" She shouts and my eyes flick open in surprise and
suddenly I'm awake again.
"Oh sorry. What were you saying?" I ask, blinking lots to
try to stay awake this time.

"You were supposed to be here at nine o'clock. Why the hell haven't you left yet?" She asks and I rack my brains, trying to figure out what on earth she is talking about. I glance over at the clock, its ten minutes past nine.

"Was I. I mean I'm about to." I say quickly, grabbing last night clothes hoping that she will explain when I get there.

"Oh you have forgotten, well thank you very much!" She says sarcastically before continuing.

"I tried calling last night to remind you but you didn't answer the bloody phone!" *I'm still none the wiser?*

"Look sorry, we ended up going out..." I start to explain but she interrupts before I can finish.

"Well that explains it then! Does that mean that you're too hung over to take me then?" She asks obviously getting crosser with every one of my responses.

"No, I'll be there as quick as I can. I'll call you when I'm coming into your road." I assure her as I jump out of bed and hang up.

Dick rolls over, winks at me and pleads "Come back to bed, the kids are all out, let's make the most of it. Don't rush off."

"Oh I can't, I forgot, I've promised to take my Mum somewhere and I'm late." I update him, as I pull on my socks, whilst brushing my teeth and nearly fall over because I'm still so sleepy.

"Where? Your Mother never usually gets out of bed until at least ten o'clock?" He asks and he's right, she is a bit nocturnal - she goes to bed at one or two every night and so subsequently wakes up late every morning.

"Well, that's just it! I can't bloody remember, I must have been multi-tasking when she asked me." I confess.

"Oh how funny, that'll teach you! Have fun!" He laughs lazily, as he rolls over and pulls the duvet around his shoulders. *I am SO jealous, the bastard!*

Mental note - To pay more attention to what I agree to!

I grab some wipes and my make-up bag as I run out of the door and drive to Mums, phoning her along the way, still perplexed at where we're off to. *How can I not remember this whole conversation?* I pull up outside, bib and she rushes out to car. God, she's ready, it *must* be important! She gets in and frowns a 'you're not in my good books' kind of frown.

"Right, where are we going again?" I ask, trying to pretend that I am unsure of the address.

"So you did forget!" She rightly states, less cross now that we are face to face.

"Well, maybe?" I wince and smile at her.

"You said that you'd take me to the sales!" She says and I instantly picture Dick lying asleep in bed, in a peaceful house and wish that I could be there instead I can picture trawling around the busy shops.

"You told me that you'd take me and that I HAD to be ready by nine o'clock, otherwise I'd be in trouble." She says, obviously very pleased with herself for fulfilling her end of the bargain and I feel a pissed off that she has tricked me to rush about *just* to go sale shopping.

"Did I?" I question, still unable to recall any of this. *I hate shopping, why would I have arrange it to last a whole day?*

We drive to the shops and pull up in the car park just as Mums phone rings, it's Patsy. I hear her speaking, as Mum turns to me looking slightly embarrassed.

"What?" I mime at her, raising my arms and shrugging. And as I hear the conversation unfold, it turns out that it's not me that's promised to take her to the sales at all. *Hurray, I'm not going mad!* It's Patsy and she's at Mums house wondering why she's not there and Dad has absolutely no clue as to what's happening and so can't offer any assistance. They agree that she will come and meet us and that she will drop her back if I want to go home.

"Oh sorry Eva." Mum says quietly.

"Oh well, I'm up and about now!" I say, feeling cross and hung-over but trying not to show it.

"Why don't you join us for a while then. It'll be fun!" She says, obviously very pleased at the thought of us both spending the day with her, doing her favourite activity... shopping!

"I'll have a quick look around." I give in, rolling my eyes and feeling a bit bedraggled, wishing that I had jumped in the shower before rushing out.

We start in the cafe before tackling the shops, I need something to eat and despite the fact that I can still taste last night's curry, I am starving. As we walk around the shops I call Mercy and explain what's happened, agreeing before hanging up that I will pick the boys up after lunch. *Dick has got off lightly yet again!* So a little after half past ten, I call him and give him a list of jobs that need doing. He laughs at the mix up from this morning, whilst gloating about what a lovely lie in he's had and enquiries whether it's curry night again tonight, being that the boys missed out last night and I tell him a definite 'no'. *But I'm pretty sure that I could waver on this decision as the day goes on.*

After an hour, we're only in our third shop and so I tell Mum and Patsy that I'll have to make a move to pick the kids up and as I'm talking to Mum, I notice just behind her is one of Henrys school Dads. He doesn't spot me. I look to see whether he's with his wife and am about to call out to say 'hello' when, to my absolute horror I see that he's not with his wife but with a teacher, from Lloyds year. *Don't get carried away, this is how rumours start! They could just be friends!* I duck down, to try to hide and my Mum looks at me as though I've gone mad.

"What are you doing?" She asks, looking at me funnily.

"Shhh! Stay there, don't move." I warn her, as I shift her to the left a bit.

"Who are you spying on now for god's sake?" She asks rather too loudly.

"Belt up!" I instruct her harshly, holding a finger over my mouth to signal my instruction again and she gives me an evil stare.

I watch the pair, laughing and joking. They're flirting and it seems a bit inappropriate behaviour to me. Then I look down and see that are holding hands inside her coat pocket... in broad daylight for the whole world to see! *Oh god, I wish that I could 'unsee' this!* At this point my Mum starts to get a little annoyed because she has no idea what I'm looking at and the suspense is killing her!

"At least tell me who you're spying on then!" She orders bossily.

I can see them coming towards me and just know that they will spot me if I stay where I am and so, without thinking I jump inside a clothes rail, knocking the whole thing on its side which takes out a few of the other shoppers and creates such a scene. The staff run over and attempt to help everyone up but as I lie on the ground looking up, the first person I see is 'The Dad'. I look to his left and the second person I see is 'The Teacher'. Then, to really blow my cover the next thing that I do is stare directly at the pairs hands, which they immediately release themselves from each other's clasp while I try to pretend to have seen nothing. For a moment, everything happens in slow motion and I think I've got away with it, until I hear Mums voice penetrate my thoughts.

"Bloody hell Eva!" She shouts, staring at me in disbelief that I could be so clumsy.

"What the hell has just happened? One minute you were using me as a pillar to hide behind, the next you were on the bloody floor?!" She says, still talking at high volume as I watch the pair scurry off awkwardly, safe in the knowledge that they now know that I know their little secret and I slump back onto the floor. *Thanks Mum!*

I pop in for a cup of tea when I collect the boys from Mercy's and listen to their stories about what they've been doing and the games that they have played and I tell her all about my morning.

She, as usual finds it all very amusing and expresses her relief that she was at home babysitting and not a part of it all. I tell her how worried I am that I will put my foot in it with 'The Wife', if I bump into her on the school run and she make a helpful suggestion.

"Why don't you look on social media? Have a look and see whether her status shows her as married or not" She says, passing me my mobile.

"That way, you won't have to avoid any of them if it shows up as being single." She continues helpfully.

"Yeah, you're right." I agree, opening the app up on my phone and typing in 'The Wife's' name.

"It says 'married'. Oh shit, I hate this sort of thing!" I say disappointed, scrolling through the recent photographs of her and her family on a recent holiday, looking happy. Oh poor things, what will it do to them?!

"It's not your problem, just forget you ever saw anything!" Mercy suggests.

"Oh I know you're right! This is going to be *so* awkward!" I say, pulling a face, as Lloyd walks in.

"Were you just talking about Duncan's Dad?" He asks inquizically.

Shit!

"No darlin' we were talking about someone that Aunty-M knows." I create an instant lie to try to hide the truth and am surprised with my own speed.

"Really? I though you said that you saw him and Mrs..."

"No!" I interrupt him before he can say her name and he jumps at my tone.

"Ah right sweaty pants, so-rry." He apologises although it's clear to see that he doesn't know why.

"It's just that Duncan said that he went to her house the other day that's all. Which is just weird if you ask me - why would you want to go to your teachers house?" He says, looking puzzled as he tries to figure it out why his friend ('The Dad's son) would be making home visits to a teacher?

"Go and pack your stuff up because we're leaving in a minute." I instruct him, trying to brush the whole conversation under the carpet . *I really don't want to be dragged into all of this!* I then call out to others to do the same, leaving me to speak to Mercy alone in hushed tones. She advises not to mention anything to 'The Wife' yet and see how it pans out. Hopefully me seeing them may even be enough to bring a close to their relationship anyway.
The next day as I wrestle with my conscience about whether 'to tell or not to tell'. I check her status again, nothing has changed. The next day I do the same and see that she has uploaded some family photos of them all smiling wearing silly hats and pray that this means he has ended it with the other women. But a week later as I sign into my account, I notice a comment from 'The Wife', saying:

'I just wanted to let the world know that I am now single. I have asked my EX husband to leave our family home as he is a liar, a cheat and a home wrecker!
Our children are as mortified as I am to have discovered that he has been having sex with one of their teachers for the last four months!
Nice hey?! I won't mention her name on here but have lodged a formal complaint against her with the school and so hopefully she'll get what's coming to her too!
The reason that I am posting this on social media is to request that you ask your child not to be mean to mine, if they hear something in the playground. They need all of the support they can get at the moment and are struggling with their Dad not being here.
My final ask of you all is - should I ever be so stupid as to consider taking my EX husband back, you all remind me of how I'm feeling right now and tell me not to be a stupid bitch!
Our children deserve better.... I deserve better!'

Wow! Shit!
I automatically call Mercy straight away, to update her, who's initial response is "Oh no, it wasn't Lloyd that said something was it?"

With that, I feel sick to the pit of my stomach. "Oh don't! I bloody hope not!"

"I was joking!" She laughs but I can't laugh along.

"What if it was?" I say, honestly worried now. Oh god what did he hear the other day? I know that he wouldn't intentionally hurt someone's feelings but he could have unintentionally said something that he didn't realise the consequences of.. oohhh Me and my big mouth! Then she'll know that I knew too and will be cross that I didn't say anything..."

"Listen, get a grip! It wasn't Lloyd! And even if it was, they were in the wrong, not him he's just an innocent child or you, you knew nothing! You didn't cause this, he did when he forgot that he had a family at home and only thought about his dick!" She assures me and I feel better already but she continues her therapy until she senses that I am totally calm again.

"And you obviously didn't feel that it was your place to say anything either, so don't beat yourself up! I'm sure she's got a lot more on her plate than worrying whether or not you knew. For all she knows, half the world could have known!" She points out and I know she's right. She's always right with her advise!

Mental note - To try to stop with my guilt thing.. everything is not always my fault!

When I hang up, I decide to run it past Lloyd anyway just to be sure. I approach the conversation whist loading the dishwasher, so that it looks as though I'm only asking as it has just popped up in my head. The subject instantly angers him.

"You know the other day, when we were talking about Duncan's Dad."

"Oh my god, you told *me* to drop this the other day and now *you're* bringing it up again Mum?!   Get over it, he went to a teachers house, so what?   Cole's Mum's friends with Mr. Peter and he goes to their house, it's normal for some people you know."   He assures me and I have to admit that I have never been so pleased to hear a sarcastic reply!   *Thank god!* All night I toy with the idea of commenting on her status and then decide not to, in fear of writing something that may make her suspicions or look as though I am being two faced later on if she ever finds out that I knew.   I still feel bad for not telling her because if the shoe were on the other foot, I'd like to be told... but then again, maybe not by an almost stranger   But it's a hard one, you never know how a women scorned may react.   I have to say though, that I'm very impressed with how she reacted to the whole thing.. no-one needs any further explanation!

I continue scrolling down the social media site being generally nosey, reading little poems and looking at other peoples photos.   Most of which are 'pouty selfies', as I like to refer to them as.   It never ceases to amuse me the angles that some people photograph themselves at, in order to get their pouts exactly as they have been practicing since they were old enough to have a camera and all in the vain attempt to look fifteen again.   If only they knew how ridiculously false they look and my god, they look even more ridiculous when you see them posing for them, with the camera held high, to the side etc. snapping away a hundred times so that they can filter through the good and bad and find the perfect one of themselves!   *When did everyone get so vain?!*   I myself can honestly say that, unless VERY drunk and within a group, I have never taken my own 'pouty selfie' and never will.   *If I start, feel free to shoot me!*

Some 'pouty selfies' though I do find amusing, for instance those taken by my friend Sadie.   She must upload on average, at least five photos or more of herself on a daily basis, all in different locations around her home or wherever out and about.   She even has a 'Selfie Folder' into which all of these photos are stored, I think she's secretly trying to break a world record.   Sometimes there are so many photos of her, that I jokingly rename the app 'Sade-book'.

Later that night, as I tell Dick about what 'The Wife' wrote and we both express our sadness for both her and the couple's children and make a pact to always consider our children in everything we do.   And later that evening, when I go up to check on them I squeeze them all a bit tighter than usual, as I think how lucky we are to all have each other.

Mental note - To remember to never take anything for granted!

18

It's official, I married a child!

Dick has booked the rest of the week off, he's been doing lots of overtime recently and so needs a well earned rest. As soon as the boys discover this, they jump up and down and beg him to take them to school for 'a nice change'. *A bit rude me thinks!* After a pretend struggle he gives in, much to their obvious joy! I get them ready in the usual routine, to ensure that they are not late and Dick herds them into the car, where I can hear the usual argument starting about who's turn it is to sit in the front today. No doubt Dick will make them travel the short distance in the same manner as usual, with the music turned up loud, their windows open and one arm hanging over the side, shouting 'Chick!' every time they pass a girl or turning the music right down and pretending to be sensible when they pass an old women. *I think he's trying to recapture his youth through our children?!*
It's not until gone ten, when I start to wonder where on earth he could be, that he arrives home looking very pleased with himself. "What you return with no breakfast, where have you been?" I question him suspiciously as I empty the dishwasher around him, shifting his body out of the way from time to time, while he watches me with the hugest childlike grin on his face.
"Well. I thought...." He pauses dramatically to add to the effect of what he is about to tell me. "That while I'm off, I could join you in a bit of 'spying activity', so that I can see how you spend your days."

"R-i-g-h-t." I say slowly, wondering what he's thinking.
"Well that still doesn't explain what the look on ya face is all about?"
"Okay, so I had a bit of a brainwave while I was dropping the boys off. I was thinking about you, getting into character and all that. In your *very sexy* office attire and thought that today we could *both* dress up! So, I popped into the charity shop to see what I could find *and* ta-da! I kid you not, there were two bags *full* of newly delivered clothes, just waiting for me to walk in and buy! The volunteers hadn't even looked n them. See, it's fate!" He announces, obviously pleased with himself.
"You are weird you know!" I tell him, unable to stop myself from smiling at his dopey looking face.
"Well, let's have a look then." I suggest and with that he disappears excitedly back out to the car boot, returning with the two black sacks..
"Jesus Christ! And dare I ask how much these cost?" I ask, staring at the bags in disbelief, as he begins to pull items out of them.
"Well.. they were an absolute bloody bargain! All of these, for just twenty quid!" He reveals, pointing at the bags, still *really* excited. *Hhhmmm, I'm not sure whether that really sounds like a bargain to me?*
"I bet the shop was glad that you've had a day off! Come on then, let's have a look." I say trying to keep an open mind, as he rummages about.
He begins pulling items out. The first item is a balaclava, which I dismiss. *We're not robbing a bank for God's sake!* The second item is a long rain mac, I tell him that he'll look like a flasher in and so this is also a 'no' too. The next item takes me aback a bit, is a pink women's turban with pink feathers at the front.
I eye it up and wonder what I would wear it with, just as Dick pulls out a sparkly dress, pink at the top and merging into a creamy colour at the bottom.

Actually it's quite nice... not to go to the shops in but as a fancy dress outfit. Then he pulls out some pink feather clip-on earring that he informs would should accompany the outfit.

"That's yours all sorted then. What do you reckon?" Dicks asks with a satisfied look on his face.

"Where exactly are you envisaging us going for our little 'spy trip'?" I ask, totally shocked that he isn't joking. "A Bollywood film set?"

"Oh come on, we could go quite far away. No-one would recognise us. It'll be fun!" He pleads.

"So if I'm wearing this, what are you going to wear? You're not getting away with anything less... garey!" I tell him, wondering whether it's just me that he's considering dressing up like a kipper or whether he's getting involved to this extent too.

"De'dar! Look at this baby!" He says nearly exploding, as he pulls his outfit from the bag, as a few other hats and glittery tops fall out with it.

"O-h m-y g-o-d! What are you coming as! My pimp?!" I ask, laughing my head off now as I study the white tuxedo with pink handkerchief, pink dicky bow tie and pink turban that matches my own but without the feathers.

"It's bloody brilliant isn't it!" He says already stripping his clothes off and chucking them around the kitchen, eager to try it all on.

"You really are serious aren't you?" I say, hoping that he'll change his mind and realise that this is just silly once he can physically see himself in the mirror.

"Come on! You've only been half heartedly dressing up until now.. this is the *real deal!*" He informs me, whilst fastening the belt of his trousers and posing at his reflection in the mirror.

"I think you've lost the plot!" I laugh.

"See, I make you laugh every day... you're living the dream with me!" He laughs too.

"It's official... I have married a child!" I say as I go upstairs to reluctantly try my outfit on too.

It's slightly too long and hangs just above my feet but other than that, it fits. *Oh bugger!* Just as I'm contemplating lying to Dick and telling him that it' too small, to put an end to this silliness, he enters the bedroom.

"Wow, it looks great! You look great!" He exclaims, slightly too surprised for my liking as I hang the earrings onto my lobes. *God they're heavy!*

"It's broad daylight though Dick, I'm sure this is evening wear! Can't we just get changed and go for a nice lunch somewhere?" I ask, eyeing him up and down and noticing that he looks rather dashing in his outfit too.

"Come on, it'll be fun!" He insists, taking my hand and pulling me down the stairs.

"Oh okay" I agree reluctantly, before insisting "but I'm not putting my top notch on until we get wherever we're going and neither are you, in case anyone sees us! And most importantly, we *have* to be back in time to get changed before we pick the kids up, they'd die if we went up the school like this!"

"Yeah, yeah!" He laughs, raising his eyebrows as though I'm nagging him. "Come on let's go."

I practically run to the car, head down, so that the neighbours won't see me but Dick doesn't unlock it straight away, instead he locks the front door and waves the keys at me, joking that he could leave me out here all day if he likes. I scour at him and stamp my feel like an unimpressed child and eventually he opens the car so that I can get in. We head off and I have to admit that I'm nervous. I plead with him to turn the car around so that we can go back home, telling him what a stupid idea this is but he doesn't listen, instead it makes him laugh louder and louder each time I open my mouth.

After an hour's drive, we pull up in the car park. I haven't been to this particular district for a long time and had hoped that the next visit would be to go clothes shopping and then for dinner somewhere or to walk up the pier, eating fish and chips or ice-cream. But alas, instead today I will be mainly trying to hide from the glare of the holiday makers and day-trippers, while they wonder what the hell we have come as! I move the sun visor down and look at my reflection whilst arranging my turban, as Dick does the same next to me and when we have both finished, we look at each other and fall about laughing.

"God, look at the state of us both! Shall we just go home?" I suggest but he's still having none of it.

"No come on, it'll be a laugh! And you'll get lots of ammo for your book." He says, trying to convince me that he's being helpful.

Mental note - To ask Rose whether Dick or anyone else in the family had a bit of a fetish for dressing up when he was younger... this is quite weird behaviour if you ask me!

He's the first out of the car and after a few minutes of waiting, comes around to my side to open the door sensing that otherwise I might just stay there. As we walk through the busy streets towards the sea front I take hold of his hand for protection against the stares that we are already receiving. We pass one old couple who I hear talking about us and so glance up at Dick, to see whether he has heard too and can tell by the look on his face that he has but is totally unbothered by it... if anything, he's actually *really* enjoying himself! At which point I try to convince myself to embrace this too, it may end up being quite liberating.. if we don't get lynched along the way! We walk enjoying the sunshine and sea air, occasionally nipping in to shops and laughing about the people's reactions as we leave and just after twelve o'clock, I suggest that we stop for lunch.

"Do you know that this has been voted the third happiest city in the UK?" Dick asks. *What a random fact?!*
"No, I didn't but I can imagine that lots of people have pissed themselves laughing today - seeing us two!"
"No, I think we fit in quite well here and you know what the best part of this outfit is don't you?" He asks, with a cheeky little grin on his face.
"No, what?" I answer confused.
"We can go for a curry!" He says brightly.
"Don't you think they might be offended by our costumes though?" I asked, slightly worried.
"No way, Indian people have a sense of humour too you know! They'll love it! Not only that it'll probably be empty on a Thursday lunchtime. We may even get a discount for making an effort! I know just the place too" He insists laughing and takes me to a restaurant called 'Planet India', who's exterior is painted the same shade of pink as our outfits and the charms bunting in the windows is not dissimilar to my earrings either... which is quite bizarre! The place is heaving with people, all of whom look at us like we are completely bonkers as we enter in our overly bright attire. It's a fairly large space, with coloured silks decoratively draped across the ceiling and lots of picture frames hanging on the walls. There is also an external seating area too but I put my foot down when Dick suggests that we eat out there for the world to see us.
On entering, we are welcomed straight away by a young Indian man, who makes a fuss of us and admires out clothes whilst telling us how he is going to seat us near the window, so that passerby's can see how we have dressed up for the occasion. *Oh great, cheers for that!?* The atmosphere is friendly and homely, with the quiet buzz of chatting diners. We study the menu as we tuck into our popodoms and homemade chutney's and we both slowly come to the realisation... *shit it's vegetarian!*

There are plenty of staff, none of whom are too pushy and all of which individually, at one time or another come over to praise us on how good we look and ask for our phones so that they can take photos of us.

We explain to them that we are 'vegetarian virgins' and so they make some recommendations based on our usual meat dishes, which we take them up on as we wouldn't have a clue otherwise.

The service is not rushed and usually we would enjoy this, however it's nearly one o'clock by the time our food is brought out and I'm starting to get worried that we won't make it back to collect the boys. Dick calls Rose and explains where we are and that we are worried about making it home in time. I mouth to him to ask her to take them back to her house, so that we can get changed before seeing them all and she agrees, as she's not doing anything this afternoon. We finish our meals and sit back holding our stomachs, complaining that we have eaten too much before requesting the bill. My head is so hot it's untrue! I wasn't sure whether it was polite to take the turban off while I ate or leave it on and so opted to leave it on, a decision that I can't now change as my hair would now like one big fuzz ball. It feels SO good to step outside into the cool air and as we head home I convey to Dick how surprised I am to have *really* enjoyed today, it's been totally different to how I had seen my day ending up but *so* much fun!

As we near home, whilst we sit at the traffic waiting for them to change, we get hooted by the car next to us. It's Annabelle. I wind down the window, as does she.

"What the hell have you two got on your heads?!" She asks us both, laughing and pointing to the pink turbans that we have now become so natural to wear, that we have forgotten to take them off.

"Don't ask!" I reply dryly.

"Have you been to an Indian wedding or something?" She asks, becoming more intrigued by the minute.

"Not quite." I say, rolling my eyes as turning to look at Dick like it's all his fault. *How do you even start to explain?* "We've been out spying!" Dick states proudly, grinning from ear to ear and I want to smack him one! *Now we really do sound insane!*

"Just another day in the life of the Good-ens!" He laughs and she pulls out her mobile and snaps a photo of us both. "I swear you two are bloody mad!" She says shaking her head, as the lights change colour and I tell her that I'll text her later about meeting up again and warn her NOT to upload the photo on social media or I *will* kill her!

As we pull into the driveway, it is blatantly clear that Rose hadn't quite listen to the whole conversation, as Franks car is sitting in the drive. I look over at Dick and shake my head, who in reply creases up laughing.

"Great. Your Mum and Frank... and the boys are going to think that we've lost the plot too now, just like Annabelle blatantly just did!" I say huffily, forgetting how enjoyable the day has been.

"Oh come on moody, let's go see them all. The boys are gonna to love it!" He says cheerily, offering me his hand again.

Mental note - To never let a man do a women's job! If I had spoken to her, I would have repeated over and over again that we would meet them at 'their house', so that she would have remembered that if nothing else.

As we enter all of the boys rush out to greet us but stop dead in their tracks as they see what we're wearing. And as we study them, studying us, it's clear that they think we have been somewhere really exciting and left them out of the loop and it's also obvious that the three of them have been rummaging through the black sacks that Dick left open on the kitchen floor, as Lloyd is showcasing a pair of red nipple tassels, totally unaware their purpose as he is wearing them on his knees and is delighted every time he knocks his knees together and watches the tassels dance about.

John has the balaclava over his head and a massive black belt with an oversized buckle, into which he has stuffed one of his swords and Henry has the mac on, which drapes so far behind him that he looks as though he has shrunk whilst wearing it.   Rose comes out to see what's happening.   She too stands frozen, looking at us.

"Well, I must say that I'm getting quite worried about you two!"   She says half serious.

"Sorry, we thought we'd have finished eating a lot earlier!" Dick says and I'm sure that he doesn't actually think that she means that she's worried because we're home late?!

"What do you look like?"   She says as she disappears into the kitchen and comes back holding one of the black sacks and hands it to Dick with a face of disgust.

"What?"   He asks confused.

"What do you mean, 'what'.   When the boys came in wearing some of that gear, I nearly had a heart attack!   You shouldn't let them see that sort of thing at their age"   She states firmly and me and Dick look at each other in total confusion.

"Why?   What's in there?"   He asks.

"What's not!   I'm not easily shocked but really you two." She says and I instantly know that it's got to be bad for her to be shocked.

"Oh let me see!"   Says Dick, intrigued now as he peers inside the bag.

"What is it?"   I ask and grab a corner to see for myself and as I look in at all of the kinky gear inside, I feel the need to get showered and changed straight away!

Dick tells his Mum all about buying them from the charity shop and she tells him that he must look like a dirty old man, for them to have sold him all of that lot!   I wonder whether they had looked through the bags or whether they just saw Dicks twenty quid and thought that that was a good deal for two black bags worth?

"That still doesn't explain why on earth the pair of you have gone out looking like that?"   She says.

"Actually don't tell me, I don't want to know! I need a glass of wine!" She exclaims, as she makes her way to the front room with her iPad in hand, ready to play her games with help from the boys.

Dick laughs as he heads for the kitchen where he dutifully pours her a glass, while I take a shower. God only knows what happened the last time that dress was worn - some people have some strange fetishes! He then changes too and orders the boys to take off their fancy dress because they all need washing.

Mental note - To never buy anything from a charity shop, without first checking the contents!

That night Annabelle sends me the photo that she took of us both in the car earlier and threatens to use it against me if ever I annoy her and I beg her not to. *We look utterly ridiculous.. I'm married to a child!*

19

It's true what they say, some dogs do look like their owners!

On Friday morning while Dick takes the boys to school for the second day in a row, I clear away their dirty breakfast cups and dishes, which have been left in various locations close to but not actually in the sink.   I switch the radio on smiling smugly to myself that I haven't even got dressed yet. The news is on and I catch the tail end of a story about how a big corporation is patenting the idea of paying for purchases by taking a 'selfie' of yourself?!   *I mean, please, is the world going mad?!*   The next story is about an unclaimed lottery ticket that needs to be claimed within two weeks, otherwise it will expire... unknowingly I tune out, as the news lady divulges where it was purchased and slip into the fantasy world that I frequently inhibit.   Today's dreams are about paying off our mortgage, taking on someone else to do the crap jobs that I hate doing and primarily about sunbathing on the beach, as I listen to the waves lapping the shores whilst lying on a sandy beach in the sun... *ah bliss!*

I snap out of it after a few minutes and make myself a cup of tea before grabbing the pile of crap that has once again mounted up on top of the microwave (which causes Dick to curse and rant every time he passes it, about the lack of ventilation and how one day it *will* explode and he will tell me that it's my fault as I'm being treated for facial burns).

I sit down at the dining room table, staring out at the magpies and squirrels playing carelessly in the garden and think of my Grandad whilst hugging my mug for warmth. Within the crap stack, there's a vast array of things - drawings, bills, receipts, unpractised song sheets and school certificates for things like Henry being able to zip up his own jacket, John being good all week and Lloyd moving up in the maths sets, all of which need filing in the boys 'memory books'. *Something that once upon a time I would spend hours perfecting every month, so that they could recall all of their childhood memories but now just shove the odd bits and pieces into it every six to twelve months, when I carry out this exercise, meaning the fluidity is all out of sync. I justify this as it being a conscious decision - I didn't want their future wife's to think that I am a psycho Mother that has kept everything they've have done throughout their lives, unable to let go of her precious boys!*

I'm down to the last few scraps when I find the letter from school stating that nest Friday is a 'dressing up day', with all donations going to charity and there's a prize most creative costume. *Oh great another morning of complete chaos, trying to get three kids ready in their different outfits before eight o'clock!?!*

Mental Note - To try my hardest to go through things as I get them rather than 'file' everything!

I'm still in the same spot, animal watching when Dick gets back.

"Where are we off to today?" He asks jovially and I can tell that he's considering dressing up again and so decide to nip this in the bud!

"I've just found this!" I say, waving the piece of paper around, while rolling my eyes in mock annoyance but realising that this is now a blessing in disguise.

"What is it?" He asks, unable to read it because I move it on purpose every time he tries just too annoy him.

"A letter from the school." I start and he rudely interrupts.

"I figured that!" He says, gesturing at the logo at the top of the page and shaking his head.

"The boys have got to wear fancy dress next week and so I'll have to stop at home today and knock something up." I tell him, hoping that this will do the job.

I have a real aversion to shop bought fancy dress, I consider them as just outright cheating! *Especially if there's a prize to be won.* I believe that the winners should only be the outfits that have taken time and effort to achieve. Just as my Mum before me, I hand-make every costume worn by my children (although nowhere near as expertly) and luckily enough, they don't seem to mind. *It could be due to my lectures about how hard work pays off that I bore them with the entire time that we work on each outfit.* Once complete I make them stand at the bottom of the stairs and photograph them, much to Mercy's amusement because every time she sees them on social media I get a text to joke about the it being the same place etc.

"I have a few meetings next week and so this will be the only chance I get." I tell him.

"I don't know why you don't just send them in wearing one of their Spiderman or Batman outfits?!" Dick says jokily, knowing that I most definitely would not and I give him a look of disgust.

"Was there nothing in those bin bags that would fit 'em?" He asks laughing.

"Err no, even washed I wouldn't let any of them wear any of those clothes! Anyway, I'm not sure that nipple tassels would go down too well with their teachers." I laugh.

"Did you hear on the news about the unclaimed lottery ticket?" He asks and I imagine that his mind had slipped into the same types of fantasies as mine had, as he listened.

"Yeah, I hope the person finds the ticket!" I say honestly.

"You'd be so gutted if you found the it after it had expired wouldn't you!? Especially if you played the same numbers each week and so knew that it was definitely yours!" I continue but I can see that Dicks no longer listening.

"And that is the reason that we change ours weekly! It could be us and we'd never know it!" I tell him, pleased that I can finally prove my point about why our weekly ritual is so important and he walks out of the room, uninterested. "Well, if you're not coming out to play with me today I will just have to find something else to fill my time." He mumbles to himself as he picks up his tools and goes off to find an odd job to do.

"Although that would never happen because we do ours online." I admit quietly to myself, slightly disappointed that there is no chance we could be the winners.

I spend the entire day creating the carcasses of three fancy dress outfits for the boys to 'help' me complete when they come home from school. Lloyd is going to be a Minecraft character with Hulks purple trousers, a blue t-shirt and a square head, made from a small box that I have found, cut up and painted and all that's left to do is just to cut a hole out for his head to poke through. John is Captain Jack Sparrow, I've stitched lots of fake hair onto one of their pirates hat, found a stripy top and cut off the bottom of a pair of his old trousers and Henry is going as a clown. His has been the most taxing, as I stupidly decided to make a big round body out of paper Mache, which isn't drying and so I will have to paint and cut his head hole tomorrow, stretching this one day activity now over two days.

Mental Note - To not try as hard with their costumes in future and to maybe let them do more towards them... I do tend to get very over possessive, when I seriously have more important things to be getting on with!

When the boys come in to see my creations, they are all thrilled with the characters that I have chosen for them *(thank god)* and how they look, so I'm pleased that my hard work has paid off! I measure Lloyds head to cut the hole and moan at him for being heavy handed, when he chips some of the paint off when he tries it on.

During which time John is already fully clothed in his outfit and attacking the face paints to get fully in character while I try to dissuade him, telling him that he can't get it dirty but it falls on death ears and all the while Henry sulks because he can't try his costume on until it dries (at which point I will have to try to figure out a way of getting the space hopper out of the paper Mache arrangement, without popping it). When John next appears, he is no longer in the original outfit set out for him but is instead a Ninja Turtle. I can tell this without having to look down at his clothing because his face is a sickly shade of green face paints, with a thick black mask drawn across his eyes and along to his ears, which is filed in using deep purple.

"Please don't go anywhere near the furniture!" I say slowly, trying hard not to look cross in case it sends him storming off into a strop, meaning that I will have to physically pin him down to remove it and it works.

"I won'." He smiles brightly, obviously please with his artistic skills and I have to admit that it looks really good! *He must have my creative genes!*

Later that night when we settle down to our curries, Johns purple eyes have been replaced with a sore red glow from the hundreds of wet wipes that were used to remove the earlier face paints. He looks pitiful, as though he's been crying all day but in actual fact couldn't have cared a less, as I scrubbed and scrubbed at his little face. We talk about the week that's just past, our plans for the weekend and decide to have an early night as we are *finally* honouring our promise to take Dad out for a long walk around the country park, first thing in the morning.

Mental Note - To move where I keep the face paints, the high level cupboard obviously isn't high enough! Maybe I'll put them on top of the cupboards where no-one can reach yet... I know this, as if they could Johns confiscated swords would have been brought back down by now.

Everyone wakes up early on Saturday morning and when they discover that it rained last night, the youngest two are overly excited. They know that this means it's going to be muddy outside, so they can wear their wellie boots and get really dirty. I decide to let the number picking and homework wait until later, rather than quash their happy moods by making them wait. Dick has to go off to do a job for Rose and Frank and so we leave the house, fully togged up and armed with black sacks to line the car with on our return journey. I call Mum on the way to give her another chance to come with us but I know she won't, she would much prefer to stay indoors and catch up on her soaps while Dad isn't around to moan about them and I can't say that I blame her!

When we arrive, Dad is sitting on top of the shoe box in the doorway of the porch, while the dog sniffs around outside. No doubt the reason for this is because he was overheating indoors, given the amount if layers he is wearing - he actually looks twice his usual size. The minute the boys spot them both, they call out excitedly and the stupid dog nearly chokes himself on the lead as he tries to reach them first, forgetting that he's attached to Dad. John and Henry insist that Dad sits in the back, so that they can chat to him more easily. Something that Lloyd is openly happy about... he has managed to steal the front seat from an adult! And from the minute they get in, the boys talk nonstop and at such a level that I wonder whether Dad may have wished he hadn't taken us up on our offer. But, as I look at him in my rear view mirror I can see that he's smiling lovingly at them both and I know that all of this attention has really made his day. We park the car overlooking the Estuary, with the play area, visitor centre and tea rooms situated behind us. We decide to go for a walk first, along the one hundred hectares of countryside, before finishing up with a nice hot cup of tea while the boys play for a while.

As soon as we get out of the car comes the inevitable argument over who is going to hold Wilfs lead first and so I spend the first five minutes coming up with a rota, trying to keep the peace. We walk over the grassy hill and along the muddy waterfront, whilst playing eye spy. The weather is quite mild today but the wind is making it feel quite chilly and as usual, the path is busy lots of dog walkers, joggers, ramblers and family's. The tide is out and all that's left is sludge for as far as the eye can see, with washed up old boats wedged in position like decorations on a cake. The route that we choose to follow juts out into the marsh land which, in hide tide would be totally surrounded by water but today there are just a few small ship wrecks instead, that the boys explore with great interest, pretending to be pirates. They then run up and down the thin strip jumping in and out of puddles as they go, with the dog bounding along enthusiastically next to them.

Me and Dad sit on a bench to watch them burn off their energy. Every now and then John pretends that he's going to jump in a puddle near a stranger and they dare him too in good humour. *If only they knew him as well as me, they may be careful about daring him!*

Mental note - To tell him not to do this to people in wheelchairs in future, one poor women went through so fast that I was worried she might not be able to stop with her wet wheels.

After about ten minutes, a women whom I would guess is in her mid sixty's walks past us with two adult Dalmatians, both are quite big dogs and neither are on leads. We watch them pass as we chat. Out of the corner of my eye, I see one of approach John and for a moment I feel my stomach tighten, in case it isn't friendly or if it's presence freaks him out. But all seems well.

I turn to face Dad who obviously was thinking the same but as I glance back over again, I see that the lady is now speaking to John and judging from the look on her face, seems to be telling him off. Him and Henry quickly run back over to me and I feel the familiar feeling rise inside of me... I am about to be spoken to by a complete stranger, about their behaviour. *And I'm right.*

"Mummy, that old lady just told me off and I wasn't even doing anything wrong!?" John blurts out as he approaches us holding Henrys hand tight, as though trying protecting him from her and know that I should tell him off for the 'old' comment but honestly don't think that he meant it as an insult.

"Why, what happened?" I ask, noticing out of the corner of my eye that the 'said' women is also making her way over to our bench too, at which point Dad nudges me.

"We were playing in that puddle and she said that I splashed her dog." He says innocently pointing in the direction of the puddle and as he catches sight of her draws them both in close to me.

"Did you?" I ask suspiciously, raising an eyebrow.

"No, we were just jumping in the puddles and that dog came along and wanted a stroke. So I stopped and stroked him and then carried on jumping." He informs me, honestly confused at why he is at fault.

"Actually you splashed him, you horrible little child!" The women shouts at him and as I look up at her in total shock, my jaws falls opens and next to me I suspect Dad's has too.

"I was in the puddle first. He came in with me!" He argues back and I'm about to intervene, when she continues, still shouting and I feel a bit like I'm in a parallel universe, with what I'm witnessing.

"Well there I was expecting an apology, you rude little boy!"

"But I didn't splash him on purpose!" John pleads with me to believe him and I do. John often gets the blame for things that he hasn't done and so has learnt to admit his mistakes, often when there is no reason to even suspect that he's done anything.

"Look at her! She's got dirt all over her beautiful legs now!" She rants, as she pats her dog's legs down and I decide that enough is enough, I can feel the anger building inside of me. But she's off again. "I hope you haven't got any pets. If you have I bet their terrified of you."

"Erm excuse me Madam!" I interrupt, trying to keep my cool. "Please don't speak to my son like that."

"Well he is a rude little boy!" She repeats again, while I study her screwed up old face.

"Listen to me, if anyone's being bloody rude it's you!" I tell her straight.

"Oh, so he inherited his bad manners from you did he?" She says, looking me up and down and I feel like punching her square on in the face but decided against it, it wouldn't set a very good example.

"There's no need to be rude *nor* to raise your voice is there!" I say patronisingly, staring her right in the eye before continuing.

"Actually I was watching what happened and just as John said, your dog approached him. If *it* were on a lead, as it should be and you didn't want *it* to get dirty, you would have been able to pull it away to avoid the kids. I was worried that that *thing* may attack my son actually to be honest!" I say as I enjoy watching her wince every time I emphasis the word 'it' or 'that' when referring to her dog.

"Her name is 'Princess', thank you very much! And I can assure you that she wouldn't hurt a fly. These two are the mildest dogs I have ever owned." She informs me and I let out an involuntary laugh. *Princess really, I wonder whether the other one's called Prince!*

"In all honesty I couldn't care a less what *it's* name is.   May I make a suggestion if you don't want your dogs to get dirty?" I ask.

Now all three boys are now standing behind us on the bench, so that we can protect them and occasionally people pass by and slow down, to try to listen in to our disagreement.   In front of us, Wilf, who is a third of the size of the other two dogs is now sniffing her dogs arses, something that is tickling Lloyd who simply can't help himself as he nudges my Dad and points, laughing and I can see Dad is also amused.

"Why don't you use your common sense and not bring them to a marshy country park, the day after it has rained?!"

Stupid old bag!

"May I make a suggestion?"   She responds, a little too fast for my liking and I nod.

"Teach your children some manners."   She says, flicking her nose into the air as she says it.

I am about to explode when my Dad, who is over ten years her senior and who rarely loses his temper decides that enough if enough and starts to end this here and now... just as Wilf mounts Princess and the women pulls and pulls in a vain attempt to free her.

"Being old and miserable does not give you the right to speak to anyone - child or adult in this manner.   If anyone owes anybody an apology it's you, for your diabolical behaviour, you should be ashamed of yourself!   Playing in puddles is part of being a child and I'm sure, given half the chance your dogs would love to do the same.   Have you forgotten what fun is?   Now go away and leave us alone and stop inflicting your bad mood on us, we have come out for a nice stroll and you are currently ruining it!"

Tushay, well said Dad!   She's about to leave when I call John to come out from behind the bench.

"John, I know that you didn't do it on purpose but could you apologise to the lady for accidentally splashing her dog please." I say and as he does as he's told, he tries to pat the dog but the women moves it so that he can't. *Wicked cow!* "Well?!" My Dad says to the women sternly. A tone that I have rarely heard but can now recall from my childhood. "Come on. My Grandson has made his peace, now it's your turn to act like the grown-up." He instructs her and for a few seconds I think that she may just do as she's told but instead she turns and walks off huffily, with her obedient mutts following behind.

We all sit for a few minutes in silence, staring at each other in disbelief at what has just happened, as we watch her disappear along the strip and when she's out of sight the boys come out from behind the bench to cuddle us both, obviously feeling relieved that we managed to not only protected them but also to win the battle. They then discuss over and over again how rude she was and what a hero their Grandad is to them.

"Well boys, if I end up that miserable, feel free to shoot me!" He says laughing before turning to whisper to me.

"It's true what they say, some dogs really do look like their owners." I must say that I am slightly stunned by his bitchiness, as it's very out of character from his usual mild manner.

"Let's go to the park shall we?" I suggest and we all agree. "I don't want any fights in there though, or we're going home!" I laugh again but the boys aren't listening as they recall over and over the last half an hour.

Mental Note - To take my Dad out with me if I ever need to kick someone's arse.. he's good!!!!

Later that afternoon after popping into Mum and Dad's to warm up and updating Mum on the drama (who as ever, defends John before we reach the juicy bit even though she wasn't there to witness what happened), we head home to tackle the homework and to choose our lottery numbers.

I choose: '1' As I have one kick arse Dad. '3' The amount of outfits that I have made this week *(the boys point out that that isn't strictly true... remember when you and Daddy wore you're pink outfits... but I'm choosing to forget that whole incident)*, and '45' the time in minutes that it took to do the homework this week, what an achievement.

Dick chooses: '4' The amount of days off of work he has had in total and '50' which is the amount of times he has made me laugh this week. *Apparently?*

Lloyd opts for: '24', '36' and 48'... we're back to his times tables and even numbers again.

John decides on: '18' The age he wants to be still. '81' The number back to front.   I tell him that the numbers don't go that high and so he decides on '1', '8' and '9' (the numbers added together).

And Henry wants 7.... I think we all know why!

So, with everyone happy and in agreement, this week's lottery numbers are as follows + one lucky dip:

Line One: 1, 3, 4, 24, 36 and 45.

Line Two: 7, 8, 9, 18, 48 and 50.

As usual we all wait patiently for the balls to be drawn later that evening but alas another week, another luckless ticket! *Our fate has to change soon, we haven't even won anything for about three months!!*

When I tuck the boys into their beds I tell them all to dream of being in on their dream holiday, eating ice cream or lying in a new hot tub at the bottom of our newly designed garden because maybe if we picture ourselves with these things, they may come... PMA!!

20

Oh my god... OH MY GOD!

I have a meeting in London at eleven o'clock on Monday morning and opt to catch the train, rather than tackle the traffic. I also make a decision to do something that I've never done before, take my laptop. *What a perfect opportunity to write uninterrupted, I don't know why I haven't thought of it before?!* I drop the boys off to school, the car to Mum and Dad's house and then walk around to the station. As I'm turn the corner and walk up the road towards the station, I watch the gates go down and the train that I am supposed to catch pull into the station. *Oh bugger, missed it!* I've got high heels on that are already crippling me and so don't even attempt to run but instead resign myself to the fact that I will be late for my meeting.

Mental note - To buy some new smart flat shoes. Not only do these ones hurt, I probably look ridiculous in them too, as I try to study the ground in front of me with every step so that I don't fall arse over tit! When purchasing my ticket, I opt for the high speed service hoping that this will gain me some time back and once seated, I lay out my laptop on the table and link my internet to my phone *(something that I only recently learnt how to do and so am feeling very 'high tech')*.

I'm already tapping away as the ticket attendant comes over to check that I have paid, he informs me that there's a power point underneath my seat if I need it and I'm pleasantly surprised with the facilities and have to admit (I know it's sad), that I'm really enjoying myself! *This is multi-tasking at its finest!* But way too soon the journey's over and it's time to pack up. By the skin of my teeth, I arrive on time to my meeting and am really chuffed as it goes *incredibly* well and I walk away having secured a role-out of projects which will be my 'bread and butter' work for the next year or so. *At last, time to celebrate and breathe a bit more easily!*

I'm secretly excited to board the train for my home bound journey, knowing that I can get on with my novel again - it's *so* close to being finished now that I just can't wait to complete it! I'm really excited about the next phase of this roller coaster and the prospect of having it published.

But as I start tapping away lost in my own world, the train gets busier and busier and I find myself only half concentrating as I am getting distracted and nosily listening into parts of other peoples conversations. I decide to turn the computer off and enjoy the time to relax instead. I sit back, close my eyes and begin fantasizing about book signings, guest appearances and such like but there is so much noise in the carriage that it's rather irritating. The guy in the seat behind me is on his mobile phone, giving his orders at high level to some poor sod at the other end of the line and the brightly clothed young girl next to me has her music blurting out of her earphones so that I worry she will damage her ear drums, whilst she reapplies her thick make-up.

Then there's two middle aged women opposite, chatting about work, their colleges and nights out. They must be close friends, as their styles are very similar both fairly pretty with muted clothes and accessories to set their styles off.

One is in beige with orange and brown accessories, the other is in blue with black accessories. *Dick always jokes that this is what you do when you 'reach a certain age', you start wearing accessories to avert people's eyes away from your wrinkles.*

I close my eyes and try to dose off but am still awake ten minutes later when the pair start discussing the unclaimed lottery ticket. I smile to myself as they both itemise what and who they would spend their winnings on. They single out people whom they wouldn't give money to, how they would resign and tell their boss to 'poke his job up his arse' and where they would go on their journeys. *God they sound like me!* Then the one in the beige tells the other about how she had been convinced that it was her ticket, until she realised she had been ill on the date it was purchased and was in bed all day.

"I always use the same numbers, brought on a Saturday, from the same place. Every week the same routine, it's like a good omen."

"Or not so. You haven't really ever won a lot, have you!" The one in the blue giggles.

"Yeah, suppose." She agrees, scrunching her face up.

"Where do you go to buy it anyway?"

"Station Road news agents. Maybe I should change now though, being that someone else has won the jackpot from there now. If they ever claim it." She ponders.

"Yeah I reckon so, I don't think there have ever been two wins from the same machine?"

With this my eye ping open, like I have just been jabbed with a red hot poker and now staring at the women far too much intensely, as I come to the realisation that a few months ago (the day that I took Mum to get her 'bargain that couldn't be missed'), I actually brought a ticket from there rather than on line... woohoo, it could be me, it could be me!!!!

I fumble around in my purse for the ticket like a women possessed and as I look up I catch the two women looking at me and then at each other, as though saying 'we've got a weirdo here'.

It's not there and so I rummage around in my overly sized handbag instead, cautious not to let any scraps of paper fall out in case one is *the* ticket. I can't find anything except lots of tissue, some pens, a few sanitary towels and randomly lots of Mercy's pegs. I know that they are hers, as Henry has an unnatural obsession with them and tries to steal them whenever he comes across them. *Weird I know?!* I am now willing for the train to get me to my station as soon as possible, convinced that if the ticket isn't in my purse or bag it must be in the car. I rack my brains to recall the date... it was the evening of Henry sick episode, I e-mailed Mum a photo of him looking poorly. I look through my e-mails on my phone and there it is, so I make a note of the date and then go online to check when the winning ticket was purchased. *It matches... oh shit!* My hands are shaking! I look up and see a whole group of Magpies and take this as a sign from Grandad to trust my gut feeling about this.

Mental note - Too clean out my purse and bag more often!

As the train enters the station I'm tapping away at the button next to the door, so that I can escape as soon as I can. I turn around and catch a glimpse of the ladies, also waiting to get off, who are still looking at me oddly and nudging each other giggling at my weirdness but I couldn't care a less. *You could be looking at a millionaire!* I nearly run from the station back to my Mums house, tripping and stumbling in my heels as I go, no doubt looking completely ridiculous! I ring on their doorbell and start riffling through my car as I wait for them to answer.

"Hi love." My Dad says smiling as me. "Are you coming in for a cuppa before you go?"

"No, tah Dad. Get Mum please. Quickly." I order him.

"Oh okay, is everything alright love?" He replies before obediently doing as he is told.

"Hopefully it's better than okay!" I answer not looking up and now my head is beneath the driver's seat of the car.

Dad reappears seconds later with Mum following close behind, panting and looking as though she should be concerned.

"Eva, what's so urgent? And what *are* you looking for?"

"Well, you know when we stopped at the shop that day a few months back? When I was going to miss the lottery online?" I yell out from the boot now.

"No. Should I?" She asks confused.

"Yes! Yes! Yes, you should. I brought a lottery ticket. Do you remember? If so, did you remember seeing where I put the stupid thing?" I ask, rather more impatiently than I had intended.

"'God if you can't remember, how the bloody hell do you expect me to?" She answers sarcastically.

I stop searching for a moment and stand in front of them, speaking slowly and trying not to be too impatient with them. *Also, I don't want to give them both a heart attack.*

"It's really important that you try to remember." I say and then pause.   "I have just heard from a women on the train that the winning ticket was brought from the very same shop, on that very same day... and I'm not one hundred percent sure.. but I think it could be mine!"

"OH SHIT! I think I'm going to have to sit down." Are Mum's only words a she stares back at me, jaw wide open and looking as though the colour has drained from her face. *Now I see why the two women on the train were staring at me so much.*

"So the numbers match too?" She asks, looking as though she may just burst from excitement.

"Well, that's the thing." I start to explain.   "You know that I always do it on line and that we choose new numbers each week."

"Yeah."   She replies willing me to get to the point.

"Well, I don't actually keep a note of them... because I usually buy them on line and so don't actually know."

Aaahhh there is a fault in my game plan!!!!

"Oh god, so it may not be your ticket at all then." She says dryly as I watch her excitement disappear from her face before my very eyes.

"Or it could be." I say hopefully.

"All I have to do is find the ticket. It's a bit strange that no-one's claimed it, isn't it?!" I point out, trying to convince her that she should be as excited as me.

"Well if you kept that bloody car clean, you might stand a better chance!" She says, not being able to stop herself from getting her usual dig in.

I hunt high and low for about an hour but to no avail. I call Dick and give him the same startle as I did my Mum and Dad when I break the news and he too is not amused when I confess that I can neither check the numbers nor find the ticket. So I call Mercy and ask her to send PMA my way, promising that I will reward her big time if it works and I find it and it turns out to be the winning ticket. She informs me that she has booked the following day off of work and offers to come around to help me look and I couldn't be happier for the offer of help. I hunt around the house all evening, even making the children join in and am absolutely shattered by the time I get in bed but try as I may, I cannot fall asleep. *I just know we've won, where is that bloody ticket!* The next morning I wake up with the larks to find that Henry has diarrhoea and has shit all over his bed covers. *Well, I suppose it makes a change from wee!* I strip the beds and rinse them through before shoving them in the washing machine and aiding the others with their morning rituals. I drop the boys off to school, not mentioning that Mercy is coming over as they will be cross to be missing her and stop into the bakery on the way home to pick up Mercy's favourite, to say thank you. When I get there, Mercy is waiting outside in her car. Henry must feel bad as he doesn't even attempt to jump in her spot in her car as she gets out and by the look on her face, she too is shocked by this.

"Any joy?" She asks sympathetically, knowing that I can't of found it otherwise I would have called her and ecstatically screamed down the phone.

"No. I know it's here somewhere!" I answer dryly, feeling a bit down-trodden by the whole thing now.

"You know me I never throw out a scratch card or ticket without checking it at a machine first... just in case. It's just remembering where I put the bloody thing!"

"Right PMA, we're going to find it!" She smiles confidentially at my, hoping to raise a smile on my face too and it works.

"Yeah, you're right. This time tomorrow, I'll be a millionaire!" I laugh, trying to sound as confident as her.

"I've got us some pain au chocolat. Let's have them before we start ripping this house to shreds." I suggest, waving the bag in her face and her eyes light up at the sight of them.

We go inside and I attempt to get Henry to lie on the sofa and have a nap for a while, telling him that it'll make him feel better but he's having none of it, he's hungry and wants to sit with us. While I make the tea, he has as usual stripped naked and appears in the doorway like Damien. *He just needs '666' shaved into the back of his hair.*

"Darlin' you can't eat. You've got a poorly tummy and it'll make it worse. Have something in a while, hey." I suggest but he's not happy and is moaning his little head off.

"I'm hungry." He cries after us, as we go through to the dining room and he takes a seat on the bench next to Mercy.

"Ah let him have something, I don't like him being upset." Mercy pleads too, as she pulls him into her for a cuddle.

"Naked as usual then Henry." She laughs, looking down at him fondly.

"You know the rules..." I start explaining and as she joins in half way through the sentence, making us both giggle. "You feed a fever and starve a bug!" Which we later look up on the internet to find that we're both wrong.

I hand her a cup of tea and her breakfast that I have warmed up, so that the chocolate is seeping out of the edges. I retrieve mine and sit down opposite them, just as Henry lets out THE loudest fart and milliseconds later Mercy looks down and begins gagging and holding her mouth as though she is about to be sick.

"Erhh... oh my god!" She shrills.

"What?!" I ask, not moving as I'm enjoying my breakfast too much.

"He's follow through! I think I'm going to be sick!" She says as she runs to the bathroom and he instantly moves up into her place and starts tucking into her food and I can't begin the clear up for laughing! *She can't bear anything like that near food and has been known to puke at the sight of a bogie.*

"Well that's one way to get what you want!" I say to Henry, laughing so hard now that I think I may just wet myself. Henry realises that he's done something funny but just not what, thank god and it seems to have perked him up slightly. I clear the 'mess' up and put some pants on Henry, telling that if he takes them off he will have to wear a nappy because his bowels seem to have a mind of their own today. Mercy reappears a few minutes later, declining the offer of anything else to eat, explaining that her stomach isn't quite up for it now. *I can't think why?* I turn on kids TV and settle Henry back down armed with the sick bowl by his side and myself and Mercy start our epic mission to 'find the missing lottery ticket!"

We start in the usual spots, the pile that is building again on top of the microwave, in with the cupboard amongst the vouchers, in the 'useful draw' that's actually full of completely useless crap, before moving into the bedrooms. Mercy is keen not to search mine and Dicks room, in case she find things that she would 'rather not see' and so instead looks in the dining room. She then moves onto the front room, while I tackle the boys rooms and it's gone one o'clock by the time that we come together again in the dining room to discover that either has been successful.

"Bollocks." I say, feeling really disappointed.

"My sentiments exactly." She agrees.

"Shall we have some lunch?" I suggest.

"Yes, so long as your child doesn't join us!" She says laughing, with a look of disgust on her face.

She comes into the kitchen to give me a hand and we're so busy chatting that we don't notice Henry as he makes his way past the kitchen door and into the dining room. When we join him there Mercy warns him that she couldn't handle a repeat performance of his earlier show and slides him along the bench slightly, well away from her. He doesn't grumble and instead seizes the opportunity to use the colouring pens that the boys have carelessly left in his reach and doodles away, while we chat.

Just as the women on the train, we speak about holiday destinations and new cars and then we slip into a silence, as we realise that it was all so close to becoming a reality. I tell her about how I'd seen the magpies and she agrees that Grandad MUST be giving me a sign! But, with every room that we search the dream seems to be becoming more and more unlikely to ever be lived out.

I change the subject and suggest that we only look for ten more minutes and if we haven't found it by then, it was fate. We pack away the dishes and with disappointment decide to have another cup of tea.

"I'll make it." I say and disappear into the kitchen.

"Okay. I'll shove all these back in the cupboard." She says, pointing to the pile of coloured paper that we use for making cards with and I can hear her singing along to one of Henry's songs as the kettle boils loudly next to me.

All of the sudden I hear Mercy let out an almighty scream and I wonder whether Henry has poo'd himself. Then she appears in the doorway, with a look that I can't quite make out.

"What?" I shout.

"This is it! This is it!!" She shouts jumping up and down.

"It's what?!"

"What do you think?! It's the bloody lottery ticket!" She shouts back, jumping up and down like a mad women.
"Oh my god, OH MY GOD, NO! Where was it?!" I shout also jumping up and down, aware that should anyone be looking in, they may wonder what the hell is wrong with us both.
"Well..." She pauses and her excited expression subsides a bit, as she tries to break the news to me as gently as she can. "It was in with the art set and by the looks of it Henry has had it and has sort of... coloured in it!"
"WHAT!!!!!!!!!" I say in total disbelief, as I look down to the side of Mercy and see him standing with his hands in his mouth, looking as though he's about to cry. *Oh god, what's he gone and done now?*
"Look, what do you think? Can you read them? Do you think it'll work?" She says hurriedly, offering up the tatty piece of paper that is the lottery ticket but doesn't look much like one now, with every number scribbled over in thick black pen, in his usual 'register' markings.
"NO!" I say, feeling more disappointed than I have EVER felt before. "SHIT!"

Mental note - To scald the boys when they get in for leaving the bloody felt tip pens out again!

I call Dick, he hasn't been caught up in the excitement, so he will think about this rationally. I explain all about our day long hunt, tell him about Henry's absence from school and move on to where Mercy had found the ticket and then drop the bombshell of the state of the ticket and am quite shocked at his response.
"BLOODY KIDS!!!" He roars down the phone. "WHY CAN'T THEY JUST DO AS THEY ARE TOLD FOR ONCE!!! I'M GOING TO KILL THEM WHEN I GET HOME!"

Okay so maybe I called that one wrong! I look down at the phone and then at Mercy and we both have to laugh a little when Henry pipes up saying 'alright sweaty pants!"
I find my mobile and a message pings up on the screen telling me that I have a new follower, ironically called 'The curse of the lottery'. *Are you taking the piss?!* I show Mercy and she shakes her head and pulls a face too at the irony. I ignore it and try Patsy's phone to see whether she can offer some more appropriate advise but as usual can't get through to her on her home phone and so her mobile instead but it seems to have an international ring tone, maybe she's out of the country with work? I call Mum and again I explain the situation, as she puts me on loudspeaker for Dad to hear too. She like us, can't believe it and instantly comes to Henrys defence but also has to laugh at Dicks response.
"Look calm down, you don't actually know whether it's the winning ticket do you and so shouting and bawling at the kids won't help." She says, trying to protect them from an ear-bashing.
"Yeah I suppose." I agree sulkily.
"Are *all* of the numbers coloured in?" She asks slowly and I can sense that she may be wincing as she does so.
"Yup. Every bloody one of them!" I state dryly.
"Right." She says. And that's it, she's out of ideas.
We all stand in silence for a few minutes before Dad speaks up and as usual he is a voice of wit and intelligence. "There must be a bar code on it or something that they scan into the computer?"
"Oh yes, there will be!" I screech excitedly.
"Right, well has that been *'decorated'* too?" He asks. And as I check my heart does a summersault. I scream down the phone probably deafening both parents in one fail swoop, as I realise that this is THE only number that is still intact.
I wave the ticket at Mercy, shouting and screaming like a mad thing and again we result back to jumping around the room while Henry leaves the room because he is getting fed up of trying to gage our moods.

Over the line I hear Mum and Dad screaming back at us. After a few minutes of pure madness, I tell them that I have to hang up and call Dick back, so that he can mentally forgive our children.   I call him and his reaction is far more positive this time the same, with lots of whoops, cheers and 'get ins'.   Before he stops and is deadly quiet for a while, before pointing out that our celebrations are slightly premature as in reality we don't actually even know if the numbers match up with the winning ones.   He then goes on to make me promise to wait for him before I check them out in the shop.   *His excuse for this is that he needs to be with me, in case anyone tries to mug me on the way out of the shop but I secretly suspect that it's so that I don't run off with all of the money and call him from a different country to break the news.*   I promise to wait before ordering him to hurry up and get home and Mercy offers to collect the kids from school, which I'm grateful for... I just want to get this checked out now!

Mental note - To always believe that dreams can come true - I wonder if our possible change in fate is due to our undeterred PMA?

It's a ticket... but is it the ticket?!
The numbers may have been coloured in but the barcode is still intact.
Oh my god... OH MY GOD!!!
It could be us... at last, we could have only gone and won the bloody lottery!!!!
I think I've pee'd myself just a little bit!!
Hurray up and get home please Dick, this is just torture!!!!
Mental note - To wear a 'Tenna Lady' to the shop... so that when I hear the news I don't leave a puddle!
In just a short while, I may just be living the dream!

21

Well thank my lucky magpies (and my Grandad of course)!

Could it really be the winning lottery ticket that I'm holding in my hands?!

I just know, from the feeling that I have deep down in the very pit of my stomach, that today is going to be our lucky day!

Oh my god... OH MY GOD... I'm SO excited!!!   It could be us, at LONG last, we could be millionaires!!!!

Mercy takes Henry to collect the other two boys from school. We've agreed that she's not going to mention anything about the winning ticket for now, just in case it turns out that we haven't won *(PMA... that's NOT going to happen).*   While myself and Dick make the short trip to the newsagents.   When we arrive I explain to the less than interested cashier the situation in great detail and with both fingers crossed under my sleeves like a little girl, I stand and wait in anticipation as he feeds the ticket into the machine once, then twice and then a third time before handing the ticket back to me, shaking his head.

"No sorry love, it's not a winner.   Better luck next time yeah." He says brightly, waiting for me to move so that he can serve the next customer but I can't, I'm fixed to the spot, my legs are like huge weights securing me in position.

What?!   What?!   This can't be... it HAS to be the winning ticket! It's OUR time for some good luck, we're well overdue some!!!

"Can you try it again, just one more time please?" I ask quietly, trying to hold back the tears as I pass him back the ticket with trembling hands.

"Pass it here then." He sighs, taking it from me once again, obviously just to humour me.

He feeds the ticket back into the machine again, while we watch his every movement, willing even more so now than before for him to smile over at us and say something like 'Well congratulations the pair of you, you are officially now millionaires! How are you going to spend your winnings?' But instead he simply says "No, sozza."

Arrhh, his lack of empathy is killing me!

We stand few a few seconds in stunned silence before his voice comes again, this time to shout impatiently over our heads "NEXT!"

With this I look at Dick and he looks at me, we're both totally expressionless. We then walk out of the shop like a couple of zombies. Outside we get back into the car that, who's rear end is poking out dangerously into the road where we had practically abandoned it just minutes before, in our race to get inside the shop. There's no race now, just absolute body numbing disappointment.

"Let's go home." I say quietly and for the entire journey Dick tries to lift my spirits, by making a joke out of how we wouldn't have enjoyed being that rich anyway but I can't lift the bad mood.

Mental note - To not get so prematurely excited about things!

Mercy can see as soon as she steps through the door by my inability to raise a smile, that our trip had been fruitless and so suggests having a glass of wine to cheer us all up, which we all agree is a good idea!

As I pour the wine, the door bell rings and Lloyd answers it. It's our neighbours, our post has been delivered to them accidentally.

He hands me the pile of envelopes and I'm about to add them onto the 'read later' pile when I notice the stamp on one of them and my heart springs back to life again.

"Oh my goodness!" I say loudly and with mixed emotions, not knowing whether to be excited or whether I'm about to be disappointed for the second time today.

"What?" Ask Dick and Mercy at the same time, whilst the kids all yell out 'Jinx!'

"It's a letter from a Literary Agent. It must be about my book!" I say, still staring at the unopened envelope.

"Erh yeah deer! Dick mocks me.

"Oh shut up!"

"Well open it then!!!" He yells.

"Oh I can't. What if it says that my writing is crap? I don't think I can deal with that, not today!" I say, worriedly glancing up them both.

"Open it or I will!" Jokes Dick.

"O-k-a-y." I say and slowly, with shaky hands unwrap the letter inside.

"WOOHOO!!!!!!!!" I scream out loudly, for the world to hear.

"They're only going to publish my bloody book, I can't bloody believe it!" I shrill as I dance around the kitchen like an excited three year old.

"Who would have thought it! From that one morning, lying in bed with Henry after he'd puked all night.... and now I am actually an author! OF A BOOK! A *book* that's going to be published! Woohoo!!!! Well, it has turned out to be a good day after all! Wait 'til I tell Mum!!!"

"Well done, I always knew you could do it!" Says Mercy, obviously chuffed to bits for me.

"Yeah, well done, you clever thing!" Smiles Dick as he cuddles me and we all raise our glasses to celebrate.

"Oh well, I'd better start thinking about the next book now, hadn't I! Where will I start I wonder" I say, my mind racing already as I start thinking about characters and storylines, while I can see Dick rolling his eyes at me, as if thinking 'oh no, what dramas will there be next?!"
"Well, you really will be living the dream now!" He says and we all laugh together.

THE END

ABOUT THE AUTHOR

Mrs P started writing at the end of 2015, after helping her Mother-in-law publish a short book that she had written in memory of her best friend.   As a starting point, she entered a challenge of writing 10,000 words in one month.   This motivated her greatly and not only did she succeed in the task, she thoroughly enjoyed every moment that she wrote, totally losing herself in the story-lines on a daily basis, feeling alive with creativity!

She chose to write this book using a pseudonym, as the characters within the story are (very) loosely based on her own family members / events.

Proof

Made in the USA
Charleston, SC
30 September 2016